To Jim
Reg
Tony Muddimer

The author was born before the start of the Second World War, so he experienced the whole of the conflict, including German bombing raids and severe food shortages.

He was educated in classes with large numbers of pupils because so many teachers had been called up to serve in the armed forces.

His father was one of the first members of Ian Fleming's intelligence-gathering commandos, so the author met and talked to many of these brave soldiers.

For some months, he was evacuated to Tenby in South Wales, as his home had been requisitioned by the military.

Finally living in Leicester until the end of hostilities.

Dedicated to my father, a brave soldier
Colour Sergeant Ron Muddimer
Royal Marines Commando

Tony Muddimer

CHILDHOODS ARE FOREVER

AUSTIN MACAULEY PUBLISHERS™

LONDON · CAMBRIDGE · NEW YORK · SHARJAH

A CIP catalogue record for this title is available from the British Library.

ISBN 9781528901758 (Paperback)
ISBN 9781528901765 (E-Book)

www.austinmacauley.com

First Published (2018)
Austin Macauley Publishers Ltd™
25 Canada Square
Canary Wharf
London
E14 5LQ

To Richard Guise, published author and friend, for his advice and support.

To the Leicester Mercury for permission to reproduce copy from their journals.

Photograph of Cold Morham Farm, Buckinghamshire. Courtesy of Mr David Roberts.

Photograph of Air Sea Rescue launch – Number 156. Courtesy of the family of the late Mr Clifford Burkett.

Zindel Grynspan's letter describing the deportation of Jews from Germany. Courtesy of HolocaustResearchProject.org

Photograph of the Welbike Airborne Motorcycle. Courtesy of Mr Ron Cobb. From his website www.roncobb.com

Table of Contents

Preface

My story begins on 30th January 1933; the day Adolf Hitler became Chancellor of Germany. This event was to lead, eventually, to the start of the Second World War and although I was born three months later than this, it was to affect the next few years of my life. This is my recollection of the terrible events which followed this memorable date.

My story describes what it was like for a young boy having to live through and experience a world war, at a time, many years ago, when life was so different from what it has become in the twenty-first century.

In the year of my birth, the notorious couple Bonnie and Clyde were still on the run in America and killing any policemen who stood in their way.

My first memories begin as a three-year-old in Leicester and centre around my home in Abbots Road, watching and listening as any young boy would do, to further his understanding of this small world around him.

Whilst walking up the road a short distance from my home I encountered a group of boys and just wanted to be friends with them, but they decided they didn't like me and made certain threats. I don't recall exactly what they said or why. I was still very young. I couldn't understand why they didn't like me, so I quickly returned home, and to safety. This was my first unpleasant experience, showing me the darker side of life.

I remember workmen digging up the road outside our house, who spoke in a strange accent which I'd not heard before. Maybe they were Irish labourers, as many labourers were in those days; descendants of those navvies who'd moved to England to build the canals and subsequently, the railways. They used picks and shovels in those days, as mechanical diggers were not in common use to dig holes in the road. The words they used were a new vocabulary which I'd not heard before, but these new words were spoken with such authority they had to be remembered and used as frequently as possible in the future.

I was called in for tea, bread and jam, and proceeded to use the new words I'd learnt so recently. "Where's the f****** jam?" I asked. The new words I'd learned did not meet with my mother's approval!

I wondered where these strange men had come from and where they lived as they were not from my street or even my town. Their faces were weather-beaten brown, from long years of working in the sun and freezing winters. To keep warm in the winter, they spread their arms out wide, then swung them onto their chests, backwards and forwards, which seemed to warm them temporarily, to allow them to keep digging. Their hands were gnarled and rough, and looked as if they'd been pickled in strong vinegar.

They had string tied around their trousers, just below the knees, which they told me was to stop rats climbing up their trouser legs. I wasn't sure if that was true, but it satisfied my curiosity.

They brewed tea in an enamel canister, with a wire loop handle, which they had heated on a coke brazier. They then proceeded to swing it around and around in the air to mix the contents. They were hardy and strong, and I imagined them living in a wooden hut with a little stove to keep them warm.

Playing in the street with the local neighbourhood children, I could learn the ways of the world. They were the fount of all knowledge, and whatever they told me, I accepted as being true because of their superior knowledge. They were, after all, a little older than me at seven or eight years of age.

This is how I learned about the mysteries of life and understood the world in which I'd so newly arrived. I learned more about life from my pals than from my parents, from whom I learned very little, as they rarely engaged in any meaningful conversation with me, early in my life, or at any other time in the future.

1936

Latest News – 7th March 1936 – German forces enter the Rhineland.

German troops entered the Rhineland, the industrial heartland of Germany, which broke the treaty they'd signed at the end of the First World War.

This was Hitler's first act of aggression. The Western Powers could have taken steps to deter Hitler from the belief that he could proceed to occupy other territories with impunity, but the reluctance to start another war, after the terrible loss of life from the Great War, was what prompted the policy of appeasement and therefore Hitler realised that he could continue with his aggression in the knowledge that he wouldn't be stopped.

Even though I was only three years old, I was aware of the foreboding experienced by my mother and father of the events in Germany as they unfolded. We would sit around our little radio in the sitting room and my parents would discuss their fears for the possibility of war. Even though I was so young, it was difficult not to be involved in those fears for the future.

Latest News – 10th December 1936 – King Edward VIII abdicates his throne.

It's difficult to appreciate in these days of incessant media news coverage, with so many international events every day, that the abdication of King Edward caused such a momentous furore in which we were all affected, young and old alike; because, at that time, royalty was held in such high esteem that the public found it difficult to understand how such a popular king, of noble birth, should succumb to such weakness, to give up his crown to marry a divorcee.

Edward VIII (1894–1972) became King of England upon the death of his father, George V, on 20th January 1936. Edward, as Prince of Wales, had proved to be a great disappointment to his father because he was self-indulgent and fond of the ladies. He was well-known around the hunting circles of Melton Mowbray, and it was claimed that a few of the local children bore a striking resemblance to him.

His affair with Mrs Simpson did not go down well with the straight-laced establishment, who generally believed that you could misbehave so long as you did it in secret. But Edward's affair became more and more public, and he made no effort to conceal it.

The Prime Minister Stanley Baldwin and the Archbishop of Canterbury had conspired together to force Edward to abdicate by various distasteful means, after Edward had suggested that Mrs Simpson could simply be a consort (as Duchess of Cornwall) rather than his Queen, but this was rejected because Parliament had voted against it and therefore, he was left with no alternative but to abdicate, which he did on 10th December 1936.

The 42-year-old Edward had been King for just a few months when he made known his desire to marry divorcee Wallis Simpson, an American who was in the process of her second divorce. Edward decided that he could not continue as King without Mrs Simpson as his wife.

Although I was less than four years old, I remember these events clearly, as my family and friends in the street talked about nothing else for days on end, and even though I was so young, I understood what all the fuss was about.

On 10th December 1936, King Edward VIII submitted his abdication and it was endorsed by Parliament the next day. He thus became the only British Monarch ever to resign voluntarily.

On the following day, 11th December, Edward broadcasted his message to a worldwide audience on BBC

Radio to explain his reasons for his abdication, which was principally because he could not continue as King without his relationship with Mrs Simpson.

He ended his broadcast by saying:

"I now quit altogether public affairs and I lay down my burden. It may be some time before I return to my native land, but I shall always follow the fortunes of the British race and empire with profound interest, and if at any time in the future I can be found to be of service to his majesty in a private station, I shall not fail.

"And now, we all have a new King. I wish him and you, his people, happiness and prosperity with all my heart. God bless you all! God save the King!"

Our Queens' father became king as George VI. He took the throne and immediately gave Edward the title, Duke of Windsor. The Duke and Mrs Simpson were married in France on 3rd June 1937 and lived in Paris.

During the Second World War, Edward served as governor of the Bahamas. He died in Paris on 28th May 1972. His wife died there on 24th April 1986.

In our street, the children sang the latest song concerning our uncrowned King Edward VIII, which went: 'Hark the herald angels sing, Mrs Simpson pinched our King'. These children spoke with much disgust that Mrs Simpson was a divorcee. Divorce was really frowned upon in those days, and no doubt this robust opinion was that of these children's parents.

Edward had been very popular with the British people and many other people around the world because of his approachable and pleasant manner. He was truly a man of the people.

Following his abdication, the Archbishop of Canterbury broadcast a scathing attack on the now Duke of Windsor, which criticised what he considered to be the Duke's unacceptable lifestyle. This was done to celebrate his own triumph at having rid the country of its King, but this backfired on him badly because of Edward's popularity, and it was not long after this broadcast that he was removed from his role as Archbishop.

Every Sunday morning, my two sisters and I were given one farthing each to go to the shop in Humberstone Village to buy sweets. A farthing was one quarter of an old penny; impossible to compare it with our current decimal currency because it is such a small amount. We would buy our sweets which would be packed in a small triangular bag. By the time we arrived back home, the contents would have been eaten. We considered this visit and the sweets as such a treat.

Another important treat was when the Walls ice cream tricycle visited our street. It had two wheels at the front underneath a big cool box, which had blue and white squares painted around its top. It had one wheel at the back, underneath the ice cream man's seat. He would pedal down the street ringing his bell, warning of his approach, which would prompt this little boy to run to his mother to ask for money to buy his favourite triangular ice lollipop, which was wrapped in blue and white chequered paper.

1937

On 12th May 1937, I sat with my legs over my father's shoulders at the junction of Charles Street and Humberstone Gate in Leicester to watch the parade to celebrate the coronation of King George VI. Flags and bunting adorned the streets, the bands played and the crowds cheered as the parade passed by; such merriment and excitement in those far-off unsophisticated days.

We didn't see much of grandparents in those days. I can only recall one visit to my maternal grandfather who we visited at his office in a shoe warehouse in Charles Street, Leicester. He gave me a half-crown coin, equivalent to 25p today, but you could buy quite a lot of sweets and toys with that amount then.

My mother also took me on a rare visit to my paternal grandfather. He owned a large company selling buttons and trimmings (which I presumed to be zips and other accessories for making clothes). He lived in Leicester in a large house in De Montfort Street. He was quite wealthy. He employed servants who resided below stairs behind the traditional green baize door. After my grandmother had died, he lived on his own, and at that time he only had a chauffeur and housekeeper, which was a reduced domestic staff from when his six children were living in his house.

Our meeting with my grandfather took place in his dining room and he sat behind his highly polished dining room table. My mother and I sat on the other side. He was an imposing figure; he sat like an emperor, with his large chest showing traces of snuff down his waistcoat. I could smell the fruit which sat in a bowl on his sideboard.

Before we left, I visited the lavatory which was a large room with a very high ceiling. It even had a hand wash bowl and toiletries, which I'd not witnessed in any place I'd been before.

Beside the toilet, standing against the wall in the corner, stood a very large heavy staff which was taller than me. I learned later from my aunt that it belonged to my great-grandfather who'd been a police sergeant in Leicester City Police.

Apparently, he had a fearsome reputation amongst the criminal fraternity, and in those days, before political correctness, I've no doubt miscreants felt the weight of this stick, before retreating as fast as possible to safety.

Our interview with Grandfather didn't last very long. In those days, children were expected to be 'seen and not heard' and I had the impression that this meeting was something of an inconvenience to him. When the visit was over, he presented this little boy with a half-crown coin, two shillings and sixpence in old money, which was quickly secreted into my mother's handbag. I think the half-crown contribution must have been the going rate for small grandchildren, as both grandfathers gave me the same amount.

This amount would have bought this lad 15 two-penny bars of chocolate or a visit to Woolworth's 'Threepenny and Sixpenny' store to supply five sixpenny toys.

My father told me a few stories of what he and his three brothers used to get up to when they still lived with their father. One story involved a visit to the Theatre Royal in Leicester where they would have a box at ground level and close to the orchestra, and whilst the orchestra played, all the brothers would start to suck lemons which, my dad claimed, would make the trombone and trumpet players' mouths dribble. I've never had the opportunity to put this to the test, so I can't verify its accuracy but knowing my uncles, this prank didn't surprise me.

I imagine that the children of wealthy parents in Leicester, between the two world wars, enjoyed a very luxurious lifestyle. Leicester was reputed to be one of the richest cities in Europe at that time.

There was a comparatively small number of Leicester families who owned big businesses. These would mainly socialise within their own circles and intermarry so they could retain their wealth and status.

The senior members of one wealthy Leicester family, each owned yellow Rolls Royce cars.

I can only remember one visit to my maternal grandmother when I was four years old. My sisters had warned me in advance to beware that she was mad, so I was frightened she might hurt me, even before I met her.

We arrived at the nursing home which was not far from where we lived in Leicester. She was indeed quite a frightening woman to this small boy. She was slight in stature, with dark greying hair and spectacles on the end of her nose. She was dressed totally in black. She didn't speak to me at all and the conversation between my mother and her seemed very strained, as if they were strangers to each other.

Even though I was so young, I could feel the tension between the two of them. I later learned that their relationship had been a difficult one throughout my mother's early years.

After the separation of my grandparents, my mother, who at that time was just 11 years old, and my grandmother, moved from Leicester to Birmingham where they lived together in a large rambling Victorian house in the suburbs.

Shortly after arriving at this property, my mother revealed that a poltergeist became active in the house, which manifested itself with the arrival of this young girl. They have been known, in the past, to materialise on the arrival of young girls.

It moved furniture and made strange noises in the night. My mother said you could feel its presence, as if someone was watching you move about the house which was very frightening. It was an angry spirit; angry at not being allowed to move on, no doubt, to its place of rest after what may have been a sudden and tragic death.

It was not long before the pair moved from this house to somewhere less threatening.

In that year, the German war machine was almost at full strength, and it became apparent what Hitler's intentions were, although the rest of Europe still hoped war could be avoided.

1938

One memory of being a five-year-old seemed to be the many times my parents went out at night and left us children with our family friend and baby-sitter, Mrs Tompkins. Mrs T was an elderly widow who lived conveniently quite close to our home, so she could be on hand for any eventuality. She was a kindly soul who spoilt me quite unashamedly, for which I made no complaint and, so it became possible for me to take such liberties as I desired at any time of my choosing, without rebuke.

In the 1930s, before the Second World War started, when Leicester was still a very prosperous city, our family could be described as in the lower order financially, but my parents went out to what seemed to be many Freemasons Ladies Evenings, presumably as guests of my wealthy uncles who all had important roles in this society.

Before leaving, my parents warned me that unless I went to bed at the appointed time, I would be taken away by the 'nine o'clock horses', but this time could be extended by some degrees with the assistance of my ally, Mrs T, to protect me from such a frightening outcome.

Mrs T's favourite sweets, Nuttall's Mintoes, were produced at regular intervals from her old tattered leather handbag. She would slowly and carefully produce the paper bag containing these treasures and pause before handing out one of these treats to the delight of this young lad. Each sweet was individually wrapped which added to the anticipation. My parents only allowed sweets once a week for my sisters and me.

Latest News – 4th February 1938 – Hitler takes command of the German Army.

Whilst it had been an open secret that Germany was rearming, it was felt by Western leaders that a rearmed Germany would act as an anti-communist bulwark against the rising strength of the USSR under Stalin, but in 1938, after five years in power, the terrible effects of Hitler's predictions, promised in his autobiography *'Mein Kampf'*, began to become a reality.

The Jewish population began to feel the full force of Hitler's vicious anti-Semitic policies. All Jews had to register their property so that the Nazis had a record of what they would eventually steal.

Latest News – 12th March – German Army occupies Austria ('Anschluss').

The Austrian government proposed to have a referendum to ask the people if they would vote to become part of Nazi Germany as Hitler had demanded, but realising that if the vote went against him he would have no excuse to take control. Hitler decided to simply invade immediately. He wanted all German-speaking nations in Europe to become part of his German Reich.

On the 12th of March, German troops marched into Austria unopposed, and no country in Europe did anything to stop this illegal invasion.

Consequently, Germany added seven million people to its population and 100,000 soldiers to its army.

Latest News – 30th September – Prime Minister Neville Chamberlain declares "Peace for our time".

The British Prime Minister had three meetings with German Chancellor Adolf Hitler in 1938 to negotiate a peace deal and subsequently returned and waved a piece of paper, saying 'Peace for our time'. Not many months later, after this 'agreement', Hitler would invade Poland.

Latest News – 1st October – German troops occupy Sudetenland.

On the day following his meeting with the British Prime Minister, Hitler occupied Sudetenland, a German-speaking area of Czechoslovakia, which took place with the agreement of Chamberlain who simply allowed this by proclaiming that this was a country 'about which we know little'. He was still following his policy of 'appeasement', trying to avoid large scale warfare in Europe.

It was Hitler's aim to expand Germany to create '*Lebensraum*' or 'living space'. Simply, it was to obtain as much control over Europe as he could obtain, by whatever means at his disposal, before going to war to achieve the remainder of his objectives.

Latest News – 6th October – Passport decree by Polish Government.

On this day, the Polish Government decreed that the passports of Polish citizens residing abroad, including many Polish Jews living in Germany, would have to be checked and re-validated. Passports not re-validated by 29th October would prevent their return to Poland.

Latest News – 16th October – Hitler expels thousands of Jews to Poland.

On 16th October, Hitler used the Polish decree as an excuse to order their expulsion. The German police then began arresting Jews of Polish nationality in Germany, to expel them back to Poland.

The deportees were only allowed to take ten Reichsmarks per person and no valuables or securities, and so once they were inside Poland, they were unable to travel further due to lack of funds.

Among the deportees were elderly people, some of whom died during the journey. There were also cases of suicide and many of those who made it across the border had to be treated in hospital. One of the Jewish families caught up in this 'aktion' were the Grynszpan family from Hannover. The father Zindel recalled the deportation.

The following description of these terrible events, recalled below by Zindel, describe the terror and absolute misery which these Jewish people endured during this deportation from their homes in Germany, and not knowing then that much worse was to follow.

"On 27th October 1938 – it was Thursday night at eight o'clock – a policeman came and told us to come to Region II. He said, 'You are going to come back immediately, you shouldn't take anything with you. Take your passports.'

"When I reached the Region, I saw a large number of people, some people were sitting, some standing. People were crying, they were shouting, 'Sign, Sign, Sign!' I had to sign, as all of them did. One of us did not, and his name, I believe, was Gershon Silber, and he had to stand in the corner for twenty-four hours.

"They took us to the concert hall on the banks of the Leine and there, there were people from all the areas, about six hundred people. There we stayed until Friday night, about twenty-four hours.

"Then they took us in police trucks, in prisoners' lorries, about twenty men in each truck and they took us to the railway station. The streets were black with people shouting, 'The Jews out to Palestine.'

"After that, when we got to the train, they took us by train to Neubenschen on the German-Polish border. It was Shabbat morning; Saturday morning. When we reached Neubenschen at 6 am, there came trains from all sorts of places, Leipzig, Cologne, Düsseldorf, Essen, Bielefeld, Bremen. Together we were about twelve thousand people.

"When we reached the border, we were searched to see if anybody had any money, and anybody who had more than ten marks, the balance was taken from him. This was the German law. No more than ten marks could be taken out of Germany. The Germans said, 'You didn't bring any more into Germany and you can't take any more out.'

"The SS were giving us, as it were, protective custody, and we walked two kilometres on foot to the Polish border. They told us to go – the SS men were whipping us, those who lingered they hit, and blood was flowing on the road.

"They tore away their little baggages from them, they treated us in a most barbaric fashion – this was the first time that I'd ever seen the wild barbarism of the Germans. They shouted at us, 'Run! Run!' I myself received a blow and I fell in the ditch. My son helped me and he said, 'Run, run, Dad – otherwise you'll die.'

"When we got to the open border, we reached what was called the green border; first-of-all, the women went in, then a Polish General and some officers arrived, and they examined the papers and saw that we were Polish citizens, that we had special passports. It was decided to let us enter Poland.

"They took us to a village of about 6,000 and we were 12,000. The rain was driving hard, people were fainting – some suffered heart attacks. On all sides, one saw old men and women. Our suffering was great – there was no food – since Thursday we had not wanted to eat any German bread."

A settlement was eventually agreed under which the deportees were permitted to return to Germany, in groups not exceeding 100 at a time, for a limited stay to settle their affairs and liquidate their businesses.

The proceeds of such liquidation would have to be deposited in blocked accounts in Germany from which withdrawals were practically impossible.

Having received a postcard from his father describing the same treatment of Polish Jews, a 17-year-old Polish Jewish youth called Herschel Grynszpan, whilst living in France, was so angered by this that he decided to seek revenge. So on 7th November, he went into the German Embassy in Paris and asked to speak to a member of the diplomatic staff. Ernst vom Rath, 29-year-old son of a high-ranking public official, met the young man and was shot five times and died at the scene.

Grynszpan was immediately arrested and confessed to the crime, saying his motives were to avenge the Jewish people for the actions taken by the Germans to deport thousands of Polish Jews to the Polish border town of Zbaszyn.

His French lawyer, however, wanted to make the case at his trial that Grynszpan had killed Rath because he had been seduced by him, a homosexual known in his circles as *'Notre Dame de Paris'* who, it was claimed, had been treated for rectal gonorrhoea in Berlin. During this period, homosexuals were being sent to the death camps, so when the Germans realised this information could reach the public, they decided to remove Grynszpan from Paris, and it is believed, he probably died in Sachsenhausen concentration camp.

Vom Rath was given a state funeral, not necessarily because of who he was, but so that Hitler could maximise the propaganda to justify his proposed onslaught against the Jews, which followed shortly afterwards and had terrible consequences.

The German Foreign Minister declared that the Jews had 'fired the first shot,' and that, 'We understand the challenge, and we accept it'.

This assassination was to backfire spectacularly against the Jews just two days later. On 9th November, the Nazis launched the *Kristallnacht pogrom*, 'The Night of Broken Glass', which saw synagogues and businesses burnt and looted, and Jews murdered or incarcerated into concentration camps. Nazi activists and sympathisers looted and burnt 7,500 Jewish businesses and destroyed 267 synagogues. 91 Jews were killed and at least 25,000 Jewish men were arrested.

It's impossible to imagine the terror of the Jewish people who suffered these dreadful assaults. Unimaginably, worse treatment was still to follow.

Then, three days later on 12th November, as a punishment for the murder of Vom Rath, Hitler fined the Jewish community one thousand million marks.

Although we were unaware of these terrible events at the time of their occurrence, we were all profoundly disturbed when we read in the newspapers and watched newsreels revealing the truth of the way the Jews, and other people considered by the Nazis to be undesirable in their philosophy, were treated. By this time, we were of course used to the experiences of violent war and death, but when we heard about the Holocaust and the treatment of innocent civilians, this was an even worse experience.

I recall hearing one of the Jewish Holocaust survivors, after the war had ended, saying that on his journey through Poland in a cattle truck, peasants working in the fields close to the Auschwitz camp were passing their index finger across their throat to indicate what the ultimate fate of these travellers would be. So they must have been aware of these death camps.

I've often wondered if the Jewish family with whom my father lived a few years earlier, in Vienna, had perished along with the millions of other Jews.

In July of that year, our family had been on holiday in Aberdaron, prior to these dreadful events, and every day we spent time on the whistling sands.

The whistling noise on the beach was caused by the wind blowing the rounded particles of sand over each other. It was quite a pleasant experience listening to the musical tones, which became louder and softer depending on the strength of the wind.

We were staying in lodgings in a sweet shop in Aberdaron and we had to climb a wooden step ladder to go to bed; quite a handy place to stay for a young lad who loved sweets.

This is a picture my father painted whilst we were on holiday in Aberdaron in 1938.

We seemed to enjoy beautiful, warm, sunny summers in those days before the war, not knowing then, or even imagining, what horrifying events were taking place in Germany and Poland.

In 1938, it became even more likely that a war would follow before much longer, and even at my young age, I was aware of my parents' worries about these prospects, which was a common topic of conversation because of Hitler's threats; although at that time, I didn't understand the implications.

Trams were a fascination for me, and I remember one experience when, at the age of five, I decided to take a trip into Leicester. So I walked from home to the tram terminus at Humberstone, about half a mile away from home, intending to go into town, but apparently the conductor thought I was a little young to go shopping without any money and deposited me at Pallent's newsagents shop opposite the terminus, where I was interrogated to discover where I'd come from.

Eventually, they managed to discover who I was and contacted my mother who, after a while, came to collect me. I don't think she was particularly surprised as I had a habit of wandering off, but I imagine she must have felt some embarrassment at having to collect me from the shop which delivered our newspapers. It was not that unusual that I got a good telling-off.

On one special occasion, I was taken to Morton's café in Hotel Street in Leicester. All the waitresses were dressed in black, with white aprons, and an old-fashioned headband in black and white. You would be served a pot of tea, with a tea strainer to catch the loose tea leaves, lump sugar in a bowl and a cake-stand full of delicious delights. I don't think you were supposed to eat them all, as it was considered polite to leave some on the stand.

When it was time to leave, the waitress made out the bill and enclosed your payment with the bill and took it to a tube hanging from the ceiling. The waitress inserted the contents into a round hollow container, then placed it inside the tube and pulled a hanging cord. It would then be whisked away with a whooshing noise to somewhere away from view and returned shortly afterwards with the same delightful noise, and a clang, when it fell into the metal tray as it arrived with your change. The going rate for the tip was sixpence (old money) which would be left in the saucer beside the cup. This procedure was dictated by precedence, which was most important to follow in those days.

In these earlier days, there was a common belief of 'spare the rod and spoil the child', so that for boys in particular, corporal punishment was considered as a normal requirement for good behaviour and necessary discipline, and even as early as five years old, I was caned by my father a minor infringement reported to him by my 'dear' sister. This sister, the younger one of two, would perfect the technique of feeding untruths to get me into trouble, from which she seemed to derive much pleasure.

Growing up in a dysfunctional family provided a good training ground to cope with life's trials in the future, but left me with a poor relationship with all the members of my family which commenced from the age of five. Much later in life, when the realisation of my unhappiness from the ill treatment I'd suffered hit me after years of mental and physical abuse, I ended my relationship with all the members of my 'family'.

Before the war started, my father was working in a 'dead-end job' and was probably frustrated and depressed and so some relief could be obtained in frequent visits to the local hostelry.

My mother, likewise depressed, was still suffering from the loss of her son Brian, who died at two and a half years of age, a couple of years before my birth. The arrival of this new son did not relieve the pain which she'd endured so, rather than being overjoyed at my arrival, this new interloper was resented, as she realised I could not possibly replace the son she'd lost.

Whilst searching for a suitcase in the loft, I came across this old oil painting on canvas, which my father painted of me when I was about five years old in 1938. I remember having to sit for what seemed like ages whilst my father painted away!

31

Finding this picture was like raising the ghost of unhappy memories, as part of a family where love had no place.

It wasn't until much later in life that I realised that my early life with this group of people was anything but normal. I'd buried all the unpleasant experiences that I'd suffered in their company, and when these surfaced, years later, I wrote them all into a document, so the details became part of that document which I then discarded. This helped to clear my mind of those unpleasant memories.

On one occasion, I was lodged out with a nurse who I found very frightening. She later committed suicide by slashing her wrists, so maybe I was aware that she was consumed by some troubles of her own. I can still see the bedroom I'd been given, and believe I must have been staying there for a few days, not knowing why I'd been deposited out there, nor if I was ever to return to my home, which I preferred to this strange place.

Strange to realise that, even as a five-year-old, I was aware of this troubled soul.

1939

It became clear to the Western Powers that Hitler's intention was to gain more territory, so the British Government gave guarantees to Poland that in the event of them being attacked by Germany they would stand by them.

Hitler had already demanded an area of Poland called the Danzig corridor, and although they eventually invaded Poland, Britain did nothing to defend them.

I was a skinny weakling when I was six years old and not very courageous, so my dad thought it would be a good idea to send me for boxing lessons. He bought me a pair of boxing gloves and sent me to off to the boxing club to make a man of out of me! I think I must have misunderstood the instructions because I was under the impression that I was supposed to start a war of my own. After the first session, I was told not to return.

Latest News – 1st September 1939 – German Army invades Poland.

On this day, the German Army invaded Poland in what was known as *'Blitzkrieg'* (Lightening War). They attacked with tanks, infantry and dive bombers, which was so effective that they advanced quickly into Poland.

The Polish forces had tried to respond with horse cavalry and were soon defeated by the overwhelming force of numbers and armaments. They suffered some heavy losses as a result.

Latest News – 3rd September 1939 – Britain declares war on Germany.

Neville Chamberlain announced his declaration of war on the wireless (radio).

"I am speaking to you from the Cabinet Room at 10 Downing Street. This morning, the British Ambassador in Berlin handed the German Government a final note stating that unless we heard from them by 11 o'clock, that they were prepared at once to withdraw their troops from Poland, that a state of war would exist between us.

"I have to tell you now that no such undertaking has been received and that consequently, this country is at war with Germany."

He concluded his speech by saying:

"Now may God bless you all. It is the evil things that we shall be fighting against – brute force, bad faith, injustice, oppression and persecution – and against them I am certain that the right will prevail."

On 3rd September 1939, my two sisters, Mary and Jean, mother and father, and I were on holiday in Chapel St Leonards by the seaside, when we heard the terrible news from the Prime Minister. So now we were at war! What would this mean? Would we be invaded by the Germans in the next few days and be bombed by their dive bombers, as had happened in Poland, and spend the rest of our lives under Nazi control? No one knew what would happen next. It was very frightening, a terrible fear of the unknown, which was transferred from my mother and father and passed to us children.

Even though I was only six years old, I could fully understand the reality of what my parents were discussing between themselves.

We'd been staying in a large wooden caravan in the middle of a field in Chapel St Leonards. I can still see the picture of this structure in my memory to this day. It was painted battleship grey. It had small round windows, and a curved roof on top of which ran a narrow protruding roof above, with small windows running down each side to allow more light into the caravan.

Inside was a small living space with a propane gas cooker and sink, but no running water. A few small chairs almost filled the room. The beds were at either end, and mine was high up in the roof space, which was so exciting for such a young boy.

Every morning we had to walk over the damp grass to buy a jug of milk from the farmer, straight from his early milking. Being close to the sand dunes, there was that salty, sandy smell of the East Coast seaside together with the sweet scent of the early morning dew. There was also a slight chill in the autumn air that warned of winter's approach.

We spent our days playing on the beach, building sand castles and flying a small kite in the breeze – in those beautiful sunny days which preceded the start of war, unaware of the dreadful events which were to follow so soon and spoil our holiday pleasures.

My parents would sit in their deckchairs talking to their friends, unaware of what the children were up to. On one occasion, I was floating on an air bed, and unbeknown to my parents, I drifted out to sea, and after a while, someone on the beach noticed I had left for foreign shores and shouted for help. A young woman then swam out briskly to rescue this miscreant from further danger.

The day before we left for home, we visited Skegness for a few fairground rides. This was followed by a walk down to the end of the pier where we spotted a high diving board, the height of which, my father said, was about 100 feet above the sea level.

A father and son act, Leslie and John Gadsby, were about to perform their daring deeds. Firstly, John – Dare Devil 'Peggy' – the one-legged son, hopped one step at a time until he reached the top of the high diving board. He stood for a few moments with his arms outstretched, and then leapt into the air and into the sea, head first, to the acclaim of all the assembled spectators.

This was followed by the main event of the day. Dare Devil Leslie, the father, was tied to a chair by one of the audience, and once secured, he was then thrown into the sea. His chair hit the water with a huge splash and sank beneath the waves to everyone's horror, but after what seemed a long time, Dare Devil Leslie appeared above the water, freed from his chair, to receive a tumultuous welcome from the excited audience. It never occurred to me at the time that the poor man could have drowned.

After Neville Chamberlain had announced the outbreak of the war, my father decided for us to return home at once, and so we packed up all our belongings; buckets and spades included, and started our journey home.

On the journey, back to Leicester in my uncle's borrowed car, we saw a small aeroplane in a field which appeared to have crash-landed. It had German Air Force markings on its side, which caused further alarm. I have never heard of any explanation of this event to this day.

You didn't need to take a driving test in those days; you just paid for a licence and off you went. My aunt took my mother out for one lesson, so then she was proficient enough to drive! Fewer cars on the roads made driving much safer than today.

Over the next few months, we prepared for what we feared most; that the Germans would invade England. So the government prepared in different ways to be ready for this event, even though in hindsight, this would not have stopped the might of the German Army from quickly defeating our Home Guard and peace-time army.

It was certainly Hitler's intention to invade us. He had already prepared barges to carry his troops across the Channel. The time between September 1939 and May 1940 would be called the 'phoney war' because nothing appeared to happen, but during this waiting time 1,500,000 men would be recruited for the Home Guard (Dad's Army). They were trained, often with wooden rifles because there weren't enough proper rifles to go around.

Cars were required to have covers over their headlamps, with a small narrow slit through which the light could penetrate down towards the road.

The Government increased income tax equivalent to 37.5 new pence in the pound compared to our current 20 pence in the pound. Income tax had to be increased to pay for the forthcoming hostilities.

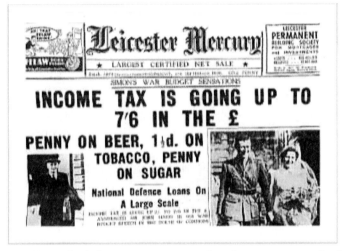

Not only did taxation increase, but the government had to borrow vast sums of money from the United States to pay for the war.

It didn't take long for the onset of total war to become a reality with the sinking of the passenger liner Athenia, with terrible loss of innocent lives.
The German authorities claimed that the ship contained armaments, but to this day this is strongly disputed.

1940

Large concrete blocks were sited at road junctions to prevent tanks from passing and 18,000 concrete pill boxes were erected in defensive positions, with small holes sited around the walls for rifle fire to be trained on the enemy. These would be placed in strategic points in preparation for the fateful day when we thought we would have to defend our homeland. Some pill boxes still stand today in fields looking forlorn and lost, just as a reminder of that dangerous time in the 1940s.

We were soon to learn that war is a dirty business. We were all at risk, every day from air raids and from the threat of invasion. Not only the military, but civilian men, women and children were also the target of Hitler's aggression.

It was frightening, not knowing if, or when, we would be invaded by the Nazis, with their Blitzkrieg attack, with their screaming dive bombers and fearsome tanks followed by infantry soldiers with a reputation for the brutal treatment of civilians.

If the worst happened and we lost our freedom after being invaded, life would never be the same again. The Gestapo, the German secret police, would be watching for any infringement of disloyalty against German authority which could result in torture and death.

During the war, we all suffered the torment of not knowing if we would survive the bombing raids, which occurred frequently. We were warned of the enemy bombers' approach by wailing sirens, loud and soft, up and down, and after the danger had passed, the siren would blast out one continuous tone, prompting everyone's relief that we had survived another raid.

We felt deep sorrow for those men lost at sea and on the battlefield, the brave airmen lost over enemy territories, and the grieving families of those men and women killed defending our country.

We were deeply distressed for the families of those men, women and children killed in the bombing raids. Almost every day, we read in the newspapers, or heard on the radio, of death and destruction, and tales of people's suffering. We learned to cope with all these terrible events, but we were scarred by the experience.

Death and destruction were normal everyday occurrences in the 1940s, so you couldn't be unaware of this war and its consequences and although I was only seven years old, anguish for the casualties and fear of the Germans was ever present in me at that time.

Most of the schools in Leicester had air raid drills. The sirens would sound their warning, and all the children would file out from school to the nearest air raid shelter. We had to go to the Wyggeston Girls' School where there were about five long underground shelters in a row. You had to know which one was your shelter so that in the event of an air raid you knew which shelter to go to. They were horrible inside, all dark and damp, and smelt of wet concrete.

The contribution to the war effort of my uncle Wilfrid, being too old to serve in the forces, was 'Fire Watching', which entailed keeping watch in a factory overnight with a bucket of sand and a stirrup pump with a bucket of water to extinguish fires started by incendiary bombs. In reality, this would have been an impossible task as the magnesium-filled incendiary bombs would be virtually impossible to extinguish; they simply carried on burning until all the fuel was spent.

We were warned on the BBC Radio and in the newspapers that in the event of a German invasion, all the church bells would be rung and other than for the invasion, they would not be rung again until the war ended.

One of the reasons for the start of this war was that Germany was forced to pay huge amounts in compensation to various countries for the damage done by them in the Great War, which meant they had to borrow vast sums of money from the United States to pay these debts. By November 1922, hyper-inflation took effect, when people had to carry huge quantities of Reichsmarks in a wheelbarrow simply to buy a loaf of bread.

My father was living in Vienna in 1923, so he would have experienced the people's reaction to Hitler's attempt to take power from the government by force, in what became known as '*The Munich Putsch*'.

Over 200,000 Jewish people lived in Vienna before the war. My father was there to learn the German language and would have known of the economic problems they were suffering. He had bought a little statue from a servant girl whose Jewish employers could not afford to pay her wages, so they'd given her this *Sèvres* piece instead. I still have this little statue to this day and it can be seen in the picture below. What tales could it tell if only it could talk.

If only this little statue could talk.

My father lived with the Cohens, a German Jewish family, known to his father through business and comprising Herr Cohen, his wife and two sons, the eldest son being the same age as my father at 17 years of age, the other about two years younger. One can only guess at what became of this kindly family during the Holocaust, and whether their lives had been ended like so many other Jews in the most horrifying manner.

It transpired, however, that because Germany was going through such terrible economic times, with raging inflation and recession, his father's company could not pursue their goal of selling products to this country which left my father with a dead-end job as a warehouseman in the family business.

Inflation, the general dissatisfaction of many Germans and the unstable governments allowed Hitler's National Socialist (Nazi) Party to progress until they eventually took power. Then on 30th January 1933, Hitler became Chancellor of Germany, quickly followed by him taking total power as its dictator.

Almost immediately after the end of the First World War, the Germans had commenced re-armament on a small and secret basis, but in 1931, German re-armament had been exposed by Carl Von Ossietzky. For this disclosure, he was awarded the 1935 Nobel Peace Prize, but because he had revealed the truth, he was jailed by the Nazis, tortured and held in captivity until his death on 4th May 1938 – my fifth birthday. Von Ossietzky's disclosures triggered the re-armament policy in Britain.

When Hitler came to power in January 1933, he withdrew Germany from the League of Nations (predecessor of the United Nations) and the Geneva Disarmament Conference. It was his previously stated intention to regain territories lost at the end of First World War, so he accelerated the re-armament programme and, as early as 1935, he reintroduced conscription into the forces.

Following the Great Depression of the '20s and '30s, factories were now at full capacity with the production of armaments which gave full employment to German men and women after having suffered a long period of hardship. Hitler's popularity grew because he was seen to have restored German pride.

During this re-armament period, German engineers developed many innovative and advanced weapons, one being the *Heinkel He 111* bomber aircraft, of which I was to have personal experience one November night in 1940.

The Spanish Civil War (1936–1939) proved to be a great testing ground for Hitler's war machine. Many aeronautical dive-bombing techniques were perfected by the Condor Legion, German Expeditionary Forces, which were used against the Spanish Republican Government, with the permission of General Franco. Hitler insisted, however, that his long-term intentions were peaceful!

Latest News – 10th May 1940 – German forces invade Belgium, Luxembourg, Holland and France.

On this same day, Neville Chamberlain resigned as Prime Minister following a vote of no confidence against him in the House of Commons. It was clear that he would not be able to lead Britain into this war with any certainty of success.

After this date, until the end of the war, we would listen to the 9 o'clock news every single night, to hear the latest news of how the war was progressing.

From 10th May, the 'phoney war' ended abruptly when Hitler advanced through Belgium and Holland, and into France, followed by our army's retreat to the French coast. The whole complexion changed, and we became fearful that we would be invaded soon afterwards.

Every day we would hear how many of our aircrafts were lost and how many German planes had been shot down during this period of the war.

Latest News – 26th May 1940 – British Army rescued from Dunkirk.

Hitler made a grave mistake in not destroying our Expeditionary Force in France, which he was quite capable of doing at that time. It was said that he held back because he was hoping to make a peace deal with Britain, which of course would have been rejected. Fortunately for us, this delay led to our forces being able to escape from Dunkirk.

The top picture shows children wearing the dreaded gasmasks and below is a decorative Anderson shelter.

It should never be forgotten that during the assault through France, with the German forces 'cock-a-hoop' with the success of *Blitzkrieg*, they carried out executions of British soldiers who were trying to stop them from advancing to Dunkirk.

Hitler's next assault was to start bombing our military airfields, which went on for weeks, with the intention of destroying our air-force so he could invade Britain, but even with our heavy losses, our brave airmen continued to destroy his bombers and proved to Hitler that we could not be defeated in the air. This success has been correctly described as the 'Battle of Britain'. His defeat caused Hitler to abandon his intention to invade us.

When he failed to destroy our air-force, prior to invading Britain, he decided to start bombing London and other cities such as Coventry, Liverpool, Birmingham and Cardiff. He could destroy our buildings, but he couldn't destroy our spirit, and this made our determination to beat this tyrant stronger than ever.

Because of the bombing raids, many homes installed Anderson air-raid shelters in their gardens, to protect the

45

family from the worst of the bombing, but a near miss or direct hit would inevitably kill all the occupants. The main problem with these shelters was that in low-lying areas the floor would become waterlogged, so you had the choice of a most unpleasant hour or so sitting with your feet in water whilst the air raid took place or, as many people chose, to stay in their own home and shelter under the kitchen table, which was much better than sitting out in the cold wet shelter.

We learned to cope with all the challenging times of war-time Britain with the accepted by-word of the time being: 'don't forget, there's a war on'.

One of the favourite pastimes for young boys after bombing raids was to search for shrapnel from exploded bombs, as these could be used as currency, to swap for other desirable necessities.

Our Anderson shelter was built by a local gardener who assembled the corrugated iron sheets by bolting the three curved roof pieces to the six side panels, to form a tunnel. He then dug a three/four-feet-deep oblong hole into the ground and slid this metal structure into the hole and then covered the whole shelter with soil and turf. I naturally 'helped' him by asking questions at every stage of construction, for which I've no doubt he was most grateful.

My first proper experience of the effects of the war was when we used our air-raid shelter for an actual air raid which bombed Leicester in 1940, but it was so unpleasant that in all the air raids which followed, we would simply stay in bed and hope for the best.

Not long after this attack, we moved to a new house to live in the country at Bushby but still suffered air raids.

I could never say we got used to night bombing raids but we didn't fear them so much as when they first commenced, but they became so regular at this period of the war that we accepted it as part of our normal life.

We were all instructed to tape up our windows with a sticky tape so that if a bomb exploded close by it would prevent the worst effects of splintering glass.

Then there was the 'blackout'. You had to make sure your home showed no light after dark, so you used black curtains to prevent overflying German aeroplanes being tempted to drop bombs in your area. The penalty for showing a light was quite a hefty fine, enforced by Air-Raid Wardens. If they saw any lights they would shout out to the householder: "Put that light out!" in a very loud voice.

We were all issued with identity cards and gas masks. I still have my identity card to this day, numbered REZH35. They were printed on card with coloured fibres running through the paper to prevent copying of these by German spies. I've kept mine just in case. Well, you never know when you may need one!

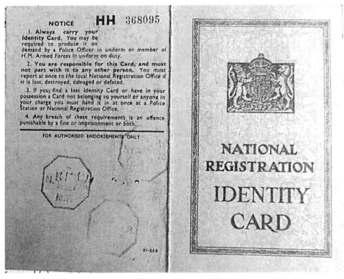

This is my identity card numbered REZH35.

Gas masks came in a variety of different shapes and sizes, from ones for babies and small children to adult sizes. They were made of rubber which smelt horrible, and when you fitted it on your face, they were so tight and uncomfortable. After you had breathed in through the filter, you breathed out which made a very rude blubbering noise. The window at the front would steam up and your face would start to sweat, but as they were made to keep out poison gas, you had to accept the inconvenience. It was compulsory to always carry your gas mask. Mine used to be in a round tin with string attached so I could carry it over my shoulder.

We were also issued ration books which had different pages for each type of food, and you were only allowed a small amount of each rationed food each week.

Because of the food shortages, whale meat was sometimes available unrationed, and I must say, with some degree of shame, that I found it very tasty.

Rationing was necessary because almost half of our food had to be imported from abroad – hence the posters imploring people to 'Dig for victory'. You had to register with the local shop to be able to use your ration book. There were squares all over the pages and the shopkeeper would stamp each relevant square as he gave you your ration.

Soap was limited to one bar per month so I don't think I would have been too troubled by that as a seven-year-old boy!

Meat was always in particularly short supply and long queues would form outside the butchers' shops. If you were at the end of the queue you may be left with just a few ounces of what was called 'scrag end', which I imagine was almost un-eatable. If you had a friendly butcher, or one who was a relation, things could be much better. Unfortunately, we didn't.

Word would soon get around when a shop had a supply of something in short supply and a long queue would soon develop.

Every birthday during the war, I would ask my mother if I could have friends around for tea, but this was never allowed as we didn't have sufficient food to spare for these events.

Everyone was encouraged to grow vegetables, which would reduce the consumption of imported food.

AIR RAID SHELTERS

I CAN ERECT AT ONCE

J. T. BOTTRILL

62 Belvoir Drive, Aylestone, Tel. 32323.

Building air raid shelters in the 1940s kept builders very busy.

Rationing was not always a fair system as those with money could buy coupons from less well-off families. Also, there was the 'Black Market' where 'spivs' would obtain scarce foods and other goods, and sell them at inflated prices. The penalty for those caught was rightly quite severe.

We also had clothing coupons, which meant that the number of clothes and shoes you could buy was very limited, so women would have to be creative by altering their clothes to make them look as if they were different.

During the war there were many lady dressmakers who, for a fee, would change the appearance of that old dress into something much more attractive.

In my case I always envied those boys who had khaki trousers and hob-nailed boots which made them look like soldiers, but I was never allowed to have these luxuries as I had two sisters who always had first call in the available clothing coupon department.

'Make Do and Mend' was the order of the day as almost everything was in short supply because of the war effort, so you had to be inventive to make things last much longer than you would normally do in peace time.

After the declaration of war (in September 1939) we all had to 'tighten our belts', meaning that we had to be restricted to much less food. Before the war I used to put a large amount of butter on my bread, but once rationing had started we only had two ounces of butter each, to last the whole week, which is difficult to imagine now in these days of plenty.

You were allowed per week 8 oz (227 g) each of bacon, butter and cheese, 4 oz (113 g) of Loose Tea and 12 oz (85 g) of lard. Meat was limited by availability. Sometimes these items were simply not available because so much had to be imported and brought to our country by merchant ships, which were being sunk in great numbers by German *'U-Boat'* submarines.

Because we children were not fed much nutritious food, we were given a daily spoon of sticky extract of malt which provided much-needed protein. I really enjoyed the taste of the malt, so it was quite a treat. There were different makes but I think mine was called *Virol*.

Most of the time during the war, we were hungry, although bread and potatoes were never rationed. When we had the opportunity, we would go 'scrumping', to pinch apples from the orchards of farms or private gardens. If you got caught by the farmer, he would get hold of your ear and give you a good smack across the head. We never complained, as it was considered an occupational hazard. It was just one of the risks to be taken in pursuit of extra 'rations'.

Our milk and bread were both delivered by horse and trap, and if you were lucky, you could catch a ride in the trap for a few hundred yards up the road. The horses knew the route by heart and would simply move to the next property with the simple instruction of 'Move on'.

The milkman had two large churns of milk in his trap and would measure out your required amount of milk with a measuring jug and pour the contents into your own container.

I always waited for the bread man to visit as he sold cottage loaves and cobs with well-cooked crusts. I loved the taste of this bread which seemed to have much more flavour than the bread you buy nowadays. Maybe it was because the ingredients were made in smaller quantities and baked in a small baker's oven.

I attended St Luke's, Thurnby village school, and because so many teachers had been called up to serve in the forces, there was quite a shortage. Our teacher was Miss Sturgess who had to teach about 40 or 50 children all in one large classroom. We thought this was quite normal because she quite easily moved from one age group to another with her instructions. She was kindly but stern and she wore her glasses on the end of her nose to add to her authority. Because of the paper shortage, we had to do all our writing on a slate with a wooden-type frame. The chalk we used was thinner than an ordinary pencil and much harder than ordinary blackboard chalk, and as you wrote, the chalk would make a scratching noise on the slate.

The one abiding memory I have of my school room was the large map of the British Empire, which detailed our territories in red. They seemed to cover most of the world. Miss Sturgess made it quite clear that we should be proud to be British because we controlled a large area of the world. It was said, at that time, that the sun never set on the British Empire.

Anyone who owned a car could only obtain petrol by having the necessary coupons, and I didn't know anyone who had that privilege. Petrol coupons could be legally obtained only by having first convinced the authorities you had an essential wartime need; otherwise you had to store up your car until the end of the war, as my uncle had to do in his garage. The alternative was to buy petrol coupons on the 'black market' at a premium price and take the risk of being caught and heavily fined.

Because street lights were all switched off during the war, travelling by car at night was quite a risky business and quite often drivers would misjudge corners and finish up in a ditch or up against a brick wall. Pedestrians also had to watch out for cars swerving on to pavements, so this was simply another hazard to watch-out for apart from bombing raids.

Before the war started, one of my uncles was a member of The British Fascist Movement (Black Shirts), which was led by Oswald Mosley who supported Hitler's ideals. He used to parade in London's East End with hundreds of others to intimidate the immigrant and Jewish community. Fights with opponents would frequently break out along the route.

My uncle didn't seem to be the kind of man, who could send Jews to their deaths in concentration camps but, no doubt, the same could be said of German Nazis who had families of their own and carried out their deadly deeds during the day, returning to a happy family life afterwards, but it happened just the same. How anyone with such extreme beliefs can be convinced that his cause is more important than human life is difficult to understand, but this kind of extremism is still happening to this day.

During the whole of the war, over two million British homes were destroyed in German bombing raids.

I have good reason to remember the night of 14th November 1940. I was lying in my bed at about 7 o'clock in the evening when the air-raid siren sounded, followed shortly afterwards by the up and down whirring noise of the *Heinkel He 111* German bombers, which flew right over the top of our house on their way to Coventry. After what seemed a long time of lying in fear and wondering if the bombs might fall on our house, I must have fallen asleep, but luckily for me, they carried on to Coventry and left us alone that night. 500 bombers flew over our house that night and the result of their bombing killed nearly 600 people.

One plane which must have had some mechanical problems, dropped four 500-lb bombs in a field a few hundred yards from our house, so that was the closest we came to being bombed.

Throughout this period of the war, you could never get away from this awful feeling of possible destruction from the bombing, or the possibility of invasion which gradually receded as the war progressed.

The war encroached into every part of our lives, every single day. It was impossible to not be affected by bombing raids, rationing and food shortages, and most of all, we worried about the prospect of losing the war.

One terrible experience, as a nine-year-old, which I still recall to this day was that we had a teacher at our school who had fought in the First World War with our headmaster, Captain Rudd. No doubt he was trying to help this ex-soldier to re-adjust to civilian life a few years after the war had ended, but this poor man was still suffering from the effects of shell shock. He would start to shake uncontrollably, which brought home to this small boy the awful effects of that devastating war. He was unable to continue teaching and had to leave our school after just a few days. I never knew his name, but the memory of this poor devastated man remains with me to this day. I wish I could have remembered his name. He will have to remain as my unknown soldier. This brought the reality and the effects of this dreadful war to this small boy.

The mental torment of this ex-soldier must have been suffered by many thousands of other men who had fought in the trenches. Shell shock was caused by the continuous effect of hearing the shells screaming as they approached and then the earth-shattering explosion. The ground would shake and, if they were close enough, the earth and rocks, together with thousands of metal fragments, would be showered into the air and onto the trenches. Shelling could last for hours and could be the soldiers' lot for a couple of weeks at a time spent in the trenches. You would suffer a continual fear of death, not knowing if the next shell would be the one that kills you. Having to experience this horror could simply break a man's spirit, from which there would be little chance, ever, of full recovery. Some men became totally broken souls, for which there was no cure.

In the Trenches

Ankle deep in mud, clawing at your feet
The scream of shells, then dirt descends
No sleep of peace, no rest of soul
The scent of death, at men's last breath
Death come quickly please, to take me from this
hell
Or must I suffer life, until this nightmare's end

These few words above are written as a tribute to the poor soul who tried to return to teaching me and my school friends after having suffered shell shock in the Great War. This left me with a lasting compassion for the suffering which these poor soldiers had endured.

In the winter-time, you always relied on some periods of snow, when we would go to the steep field behind the Rose and Crown pub in Thurnby for sledging. I didn't have one of my own but you could borrow one from friends for the occasional ride.

One wealthy family had a sledge built for about six people which would hurtle down the hill at break-neck speed to the delight of its passengers.

Ladies of the Auxiliary Territorial Service (ATS), marching proudly through Leicester, having 'passed-out' after their basic training had been completed.

They served as clerks, cooks, motor mechanics and many other trades which had previously only been carried out by men. This allowed more manpower to be recruited into the fighting forces.

It may well be that some of these ladies took part in a cricket match against my school team later in the war when I was eleven years old. Much to my ever-lasting shame and disgust, they won the match!

Essential wartime information was broadcast on the radio and published in newspapers and on posters. The Ministry of Food gave advice on how to make your limited food ration go further with advice on the use of powdered egg and recipes using un-rationed foods. The National Savings Committee implored people to buy war bonds which aided the war effort and would be redeemable after the end of hostilities. The Ministry of Home Security gave advice on how to deal with incendiary fire bombs and, of course, 'Make Do and Mend' was a popular theme because you had to make everything last longer. You would stitch up old clothes and mend anything else rather than throw it away, because everything was in short supply as so many materials were required for the war effort.

Another poster warned 'Walls Have Ears', which told people not to divulge secrets to anyone, so spies could not report it back to Germany. One poster pictured a gas mask with the words: 'Hitler will send no warning, so always carry your gas mask'. Another poster asked men to join the Merchant Navy. Many merchant seamen were lost at sea in the Battle of the Atlantic. Merchant ships were delivering vital food supplies from the United States which prevented us from starving.

I used to go to Mr Orton's farm, not far from my home to 'help' bring in the harvest but no doubt I was being more of a hindrance than a help. They had a machine which cut the corn, which then tied up the sheaves into bundles which were stacked into groups of six with three on either side to stop them falling over. Later, a horse-drawn cart would arrive and the sheaves would be lifted by the men using pitch forks. This is when I decided to help, but when I tried to lift them, I found I wasn't strong enough so I just had to watch in admiration.

Many young women worked on the farms after joining the Women's Land Army. They carried out virtually all the same kind of jobs previously done by men, prior to the beginning of the war, such as caring for the animals, ploughing and harvesting. They wore green jumpers and brown jodhpurs (riding-breeches) and leather boots. In 1941, the government passed a law requiring women between the ages of 20 and 30 to be called up to help with the war efforts.

They also served in the forces as WAFFS in the RAF and WRENS in the Royal Navy and the ATS in the Army in non-combatant roles, but nonetheless made a valuable contribution, allowing more men to be available for the fighting forces.

At home, our entertainment centred around the 'wireless', as we called the radio in those days. It sat on a small table in the corner of the room. During the wintertime, we would huddle close to the small fire, our faces red with the heat and our backs cold as ice because most of the heat from the coal fire went straight up the chimney.

At supper time we would make toast with a long toasting fork holding the slice of bread up against the flames of the coal fire until we had nice crispy bread. The toast always seemed to taste of coal smoke, but it was still a treat.

We listened to the BBC Home Service on the radio. The 9 o'clock news was the most important programme of the day because we needed to hear about the progress of the fighting in Europe. Some of the programmes were for children, with 'Children's Hour' being a favourite of mine at that time.

The BBC broadcast educational programmes during the day for schools. At lunchtime, three times a week, 'Workers' Playtime' was broadcast from factories, with singers and comedians. This programme became very popular with most listeners, but the most anticipated programme for boys was 'Dick Barton, Special Agent' which was broadcast at 6.45 pm every weekday evening.

Our family would all sit around the small fireplace in the scullery, listening to the radio, but my entertainment was listening to my mother and my two sisters discussing what appeared to them to be important and necessary matters. They didn't appear to be aware of my presence or, if they were, I was of so little importance that they never included me in their deliberations. So, I could sit quietly and consider everything they were discussing as an innocent bystander, which allowed me to analyse what they were discussing without any involvement in the conversation.

One such regular conversation revolved around our Great Aunt Lottie. Apparently, my aunt had been left shares in a few railway companies by her brother, in trust for my mother, for when dear Aunt Lottie died.

It didn't mean that they wished her dead, but if and when this did occur, it would have certain advantages. You could say they had 'great expectations'.

This frequent discussion always took some considerable time and became a regular topic of their conversations, so they would discuss their list of desires, which would include a new house, new dresses and shoes, and the many luxuries which had so far been unaffordable.

In those days, if you wanted extra money, you asked your bank manager for an overdraft and, as this was a regular means of additional funding, it also became a regular topic of conversation amongst our friends and families.

In the event, the day arrived for dear Aunt Lottie to expire, which happened to coincide with the railways being nationalised; all the supposed wealth became almost worthless and, with this disaster, all their hopes and dreams were shattered. I must admit to great amusement at this turn of events.

Once a week, in the evening, we would listen to the radio to hear Lord Haw-Haw (William Joyce) who'd been born in America, then moved to England and joined the English Fascist Movement, known as the Black Shirts, who supported Hitler's ideals.

He moved to Germany just before the war started to broadcast on the radio once every week, the programme starting with four drum beats: *'dar-dar-dar-dum, dar-dar-dar-dum'*, repeated a few times. Then he would announce in his squeaky voice: "Germany calling, Germany calling." He would then taunt us with his propaganda about how great the Germans were, and that they were winning the war, and other silly prophecies of doom, at which we would all be laughing, because we didn't believe a word of what he said. At the end of the war, he was captured, tried and found guilty of treason. He was hanged by the infamous executioner Albert Pierrepoint.

Latest News – 10th December – Two German Spies hanged.

Two Nazi spies were hanged at Pentonville prison that day. They'd come into this country in the guise of refugees from enemy-occupied countries. They had plenty of money and carried with them a tiny radio transmitter for sending messages to Germany. Their instructions were to move around the country and obtain as much information of a military nature as possible.

They were told that their stay in England would be short-lived, because they would soon be relieved by German invading forces. We all believed this was going to happen after May 1940. Fortunately for us, it didn't.

My mother's brother, Uncle Henry, was not required to serve in the forces because he was in a reserved occupation, which meant he was carrying out essential war work. We visited him at the factory where he worked for a company called Cleco.

He sat at his drawing board, pencil in hand, paused, ready to complete a plan of a new bomb carriage. He had a cigarette between his lips and blew the rising smoke from his face with puffs of air from his mouth to stop the smoke going into his eyes. His lips appeared stained by chain smoking and his fingers were stained a similar hue.

This company manufactured electric bomb carriages for transporting primed bombs to be loaded into the aircraft, ready for the next bombing raid. I presume these carriages needed to be electric for safety, rather than have the risk from petrol-driven engines.

Uncle Henry had a red MG sports car in his garage when we visited him. I would sit in it and imagine I was driving around all the country roads at high speed.

Another of the regular topics of conversations amongst my family was their hatred of the Jews, commonplace amongst many people at that time but something I found to be most disagreeable. I would state my own opinion but that didn't meet with their approval.

One day, quite unexpectedly, my dad arrived home with a dog. He was a Cocker Spaniel, coloured nut brown and white patches, and I imagine he wasn't more than six months old. I'd never had any expectations of having a dog before, but within a few days, Jim and I became the best of friends.

It's difficult to know how a person could have such a close relationship with an animal, but this dog knew my every mood. If I was happy, he would be happy too, shown by vigorously wagging his tail, or if I was sad, he knew and would console me just by a look of sympathetic understanding.

One terrible day after we'd had Jim for about a year, someone came to our house to tell me that Jim had been run over by a car. He must have followed someone from our house and, not being used to the roads, simply crossed over and lost his life. It was one of the worst moments of my young life. Something inside me died as well. I'd lost my best friend.

My dog Jim had love in his eyes
He could've been my brother
His love was so sure
He asked no favours
And his loyalty was pure
He never complained
He'd just give me his paw
He was my best friend
I'd give him all, to be sure
I cried when he died
For my dog was no more

The picture at the top is the Freeman, Hardy & Willis building in Humberstone Gate on fire, following the bombing raid on Leicester. I went into town the following morning to see the burnt-out building still smouldering after a land mine had destroyed this and all the adjacent buildings. The lower picture is someone's home destroyed in the same air-raid.

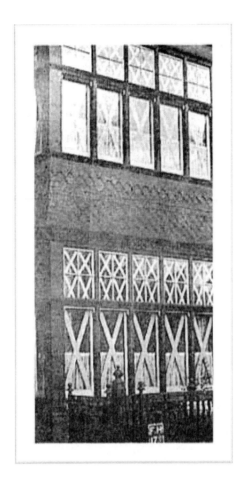

Taped-up-windows on houses were a normal sight during the war. It prevented shattered glass injuring people in the event of a bomb blast.

1941

One terrible event of this year was when the British battle-ship HMS Hood was sunk in the North Sea on 24th May by the German battleship Bismarck with the loss of 1,500 brave sailors. Only six men survived. I think this was probably the lowest point of the whole war for all of us in England. We all suffered this loss, as if the men had been our own family members. This event clearly revealed the prospect that we may lose the war.

Two days later, on 26th May, after the sinking of the battleship, my father decided he would volunteer to join the Royal Navy, although at the age of 35 he was not required to do so. He visited the recruiting office in Leicester, but was persuaded to join the Royal Marines. It wasn't to be long before he left us to commence his basic training, and I was left with three unpleasant females who considered themselves superior beings, whilst everyone else, to their minds, was inferior, particularly me!

It was no surprise that my father joined up. He was the youngest of four brothers, all working for their father in a company selling buttons and trimmings to the hosiery and clothing industry. He sat in a miserably small office below ground level, with just a small window at ceiling height to illuminate this dark office with just a single electric light above his desk. You could almost imagine he was Bob Cratchit working for Ebenezer Scrooge.

He had had reasonable expectations at one time for a bright future, learning to speak German to enable the company to sell their products to that country. But this didn't happen because of the threat of war.

The time drew near for my father to leave, and then the awful day arrived; 24th June 1941. I hadn't been part of any of the discussion about my father joining the forces and wasn't sure if it would ever happen. My heart sank as I watched him walk down the road to join up. I wasn't aware of my mother's and sisters' reaction as I was simply consumed by my own sorrow. It would be five years before he would return to our family and civilian life, and normal family life was put on hold until the end of the war in 1945.

As he was striding out down the road, he became smaller in the distance. He was wearing his gabardine mac, his trilby hat planted firmly on his head, and he was carrying a small brown suitcase. At the end of our road, he turned into another street and was gone. I didn't know if he would ever return. By the time he did come back after the war had finished, we'd all been changed by its effects, and by me growing up from a six-year-old at the beginning of the war to a twelve-year-old boy at its end.

PLY/X 104192 Marine Muddimer. My father pictured as a new-recruit.
My dad became a soldier, and off he went to war

He meant to shoot a German, and
hope to make it score
The German was a soldier, and he
went off to war
He meant to shoot my dad, but
missed
So home he came once more

My father completed his basic training and clerical course at Exton in Devon on 25th August 1941, and after a short leave was posted to 15 Machine Gun Battalion, Royal Marines, in Tenby, South Wales, as a company clerk.

This was probably the lowest point of the war.

During the weekends and school holidays in those warm sunny days of the 1940s, I was always out with my pals.

We would walk for what seemed like many miles, over fields and along country roads, through woods, jumping over streams and climbing trees to search for the next route we wished to travel. We walked in a north-easterly direction from Bushby, and could walk for miles without seeing any person or building. This was a real boy's adventure, exploring anything which looked interesting. At every turn, there were new experiences to be enjoyed, in fields and hedgerows: rare butterflies and a great variety of wildlife and birds, which were so numerous in those beautiful unpolluted days, which took us, for one whole day, away from the reality of the war.

On one occasion, we found a rubbish tip in the middle of a field which was full of old bottles, discarded metal objects and many other bits and pieces. This secured our attention for some considerable time as we picked through it, looking for pieces of treasure. Sadly, we were to be disappointed at not finding anything of value.

We would walk along the railway track and enter the railwaymen's shed by the side of the line and take out the explosive fog warning cartridges, in the middle of summer, and attach one to the rail by two clips to hold them in place, and then wait for the train to pass over and explode the charge. I think the train driver must have been used to this prank for as he passed by, he shook his fist and shouted something rude at us from his cab, and then steamed straight on.

Latest News – Air Ace Douglas Bader Captured.

The famous fighter pilot Douglas Bader, who'd been awarded the DSO and DFC medals for bravery, was reported missing in August and became a prisoner of war. He had lost both legs in a plane crash in 1933 but argued his way back into the RAF to take part in the Battle of Britain.

Regardless of his disability, he was continually trying to escape from captivity in ordinary prisoner of war camps and was eventually sent to Colditz Castle from where it was no longer possible to escape.

In December 1941, the government passed an act which required women between the ages of 20 and 30, later extended to between 19 and 43 years, to be conscripted into one of the services. My Aunt Edith was required to work in a munitions factory in Leicester for the rest of the war. My mother was excused for family reasons.

The radio continued to be one of the most important sources of entertainment during the war and one of the most important personalities was the singer Vera Lynn, who was known as the 'The Forces' Sweetheart'. The songs she sang gave everyone hope for the future, such as: *'We'll meet again, don't know where, don't know when, but I know we'll meet again some sunny day.'* Also, *'Wish me luck as you wave me goodbye'* and *'There'll be blue birds over the white cliffs of Dover.'*

These songs don't mean much to anyone nowadays, but when families were torn apart and fighting men of the services were at risk of not returning home to their loved ones, these songs became very important to help keep up our spirits and give us hope for better times ahead.

When I hear some of the war time songs sung by Vera Lynn, it still creates a strong feeling of nostalgia, bringing back so many memories of pathos, hope, tragedy and sometimes occasional episodes of enjoyment.

Many of the stars of the day would appear on the popular radio programme called 'Workers' Playtime' which came directly from factories producing armaments, ships and aeroplanes. The audience would clap and cheer every star. It was such a rare treat for them to enjoy after working long hours in the factories for the war effort.

Max Miller was one of the favourites of the time. He told smutty jokes which left nothing to the imagination. I saw him when he appeared at the Theatre Royal in Leicester. He wore loud coloured suits with wide collars.

Another of my favourites was George Formby, who was a singer-turned-comedy film star. His hit song was *'When I'm Cleaning Windows'*, which had some suggestive words about what he saw whilst at people's windows!

My father looked like George and would often be mistaken for him, much to his amusement.

Gracie Fields was a popular singer at that time, but when the war became too hot for her, she skipped off to Canada to a safer environment. Many years later whilst visiting Capri, my first wife thought she would visit her at her villa but was told very bluntly to go away.

Al Bowlly was a popular singer at that time, and another great favourite of mine. He was compared to Bing Crosby but in my opinion was superior. He was to be killed in his Jermyn Street apartment during a bombing raid in London in 1941.

Sometimes we would have visits in our street from a man on a bicycle shouting, 'Sharpen your knives' in a very loud voice. He had a stand on the back wheels of his bike which allowed him to sit and turn his pedals at speed which in turn spun the grinding wheel sited above his front wheel. He would slide the knives along the grinding wheel and sparks would fly out at the side, much to my amusement.

Another regular visitor in our street was the collector of scrap, who would shout loudly and continuously, 'Rag and bone', 'Rag and bone', as he pushed his hand-cart along the road. He would collect any old rags or any type of metal objects, although metal scrap was rare because most of the metal had already been collected for the war effort. The bones he collected were sold for making glue.

I can describe our scullery as if I was still sitting in front of the little fireplace. We had a pantry which led off from the scullery which was sited on the cool side of the house and contained a thick stone shelf, to keep products cool. Our pantry had a small store cupboard with a wire-mesh fronted door to keep out the flies. A bucket of preserving liquid stood on the tiled floor, eggs were then placed into a wire basket which was then lowered into the bucket. On the ceiling was a 'Shiela's Maid' a rack with five wooden rails which could be raised or lowered as desired, for drying clothes after they'd been passed through the mangle.

Our kitchen was very small and contained a Belfast sink, a cooker and coal fired boiler for washing clothes and a mangle for use on Monday 'wash-days'.

The two newspaper headings below are both examples of the misinformation which was common throughout the war. These articles were an exaggeration of the facts to make people believe we were doing better than we were and to keep up their morale. The lower headline was a gross under-reporting, because over 500 bombers actually took part in the raid on Coventry, and it was highly unlikely that nine Spitfires shot down seventeen Messerschmitt fighter planes.

Woman Told Officer To Strike

Said to have told an Army officer that he was foolish to fight, and to have suggested that he should " pack it up " and go on strike, Selma Johnson (28), whose address was given as Bath-road, Reading, was at Reading to-day sentenced to two months' imprisonment on a charge of " endeavouring to cause disaffection among persons in H.M. Service, likely to lead to breaches of duty."

Johnson, in evidence, denied having made these statements. She admitted she was dismissed from a munition factory because she was found asleep, but denied that she had been accused of saying defeatist things at the factory.

Trying to cause disaffection amongst the military forces during the war was a criminal offence, as illustrated in the above article when the offender was imprisoned for two months.

As can be seen from this full page of adverts, many cinemas existed in Leicester in the 1940s, it being a very popular form of entertainment at that time. George Formby and Old Mother Riley were favourites, with young and old alike. The Floral Hall was known as 'The Flea Pit'. No fleas when I visited, but it was dingy and old-fashioned.

Telegrams they all dreaded

AS a young Post Office Telegraph Boy I have vivid memories of the time when I shared the sad task of delivering War Office telegrams to numerous Leicester homes, to inform next of kin that their loved one had become a war casualty due to the sinking of the battleship Royal Oak at Scapa Flow in October 1939.

The very sight of our uniforms brought instant feelings of dread as doors were opened to us.

My other memory, again in my job as a messenger boy, was of the time, in June 1940, when I was sent, with other boys, to the railway station in Great Central Street to meet the many special trains which stopped there on their way north, carrying the dishevilled and exhausted soldiers who had been rescued off the Dunkirk beaches.

JOHN E. CATLIN
Jersey Road, Leicester.

AS a young man of 22 I was employed as an engineer's fitter at Mellor Bromley in St. Saviour's Road when the firm was already geared up to a healthy war work production.

My job was to make the elevating gearboxes for two-pound anti-tank guns. We worked hard with many hours of overtime and we felt we were working to our limit of endurance.

Then Winston Churchill made the stirring call that every able-bodied man should be prepared to take up arms to defend our realm. Thus the LDV "look, duck and vanish", was formed. Our works quickly formed a battalion.

We were our LDV armbands and our first muster saw various weapons brought forth from attics, sheds and cupboards. One young fellow from the drawing office was the proud possessor of a World War One German rifle complete with bayonet.

He was the centre of attraction. The weapon was of fearsome appearance but of little use as there was no ammo. Later Dad's Army was supplied with .303 rifles.

Dressed in denim uniforms, black leather gaiters and Army issue boots we assiduously trained on Evington playing fields every Sunday morning, and were all secretly chuffed when we reached a semblance of order.

Suddenly out of the blue came the command we had waited for — reporting to Glen Parva barracks to undergo test firing of our rifles.

After that instruction we were the elite. Woe betide any luckless Hun that came into our .303 sights.

MAURICE HAWKINS
Heathgate, Norwich.

■ Mr. Hawkins enlisted into the Army in 1942.

DURING the early days of the war I was a projectionist at the Picture House, Granby Street, and one of my jobs used to be to run from there to the City Cinema with a copy of the Gaumont British News. For the sake of war-time economy the two cinemas shared one copy of the news-reel between them.

In the evening break I used to go to Humberstone Gate where there was a mobile hot dog stall permanently parked near the old weighbridge. It was open to the elements during the daytime but because of the blackout there used to be a heavy canvas sheet covering the front at nights and you had to wriggle underneath that to get served.

To me the war was not really finished until I had a letter from my girlfriend, now my wife, to tell me that the Bovril sign at the Clock Tower was lit up again.

MAX E. LIEVERS,
Leicester.

Every family with relatives serving in the forces dreaded the sight of the Telegraph Boy approaching their home on his red bicycle, as the telegram may contain the name of your relative followed by 'We regret to inform you', 'killed in action', 'missing, presumed dead' and other such brief announcements.

1942

Latest News – The Yanks arrived…

In January 1942, the Yanks (American soldiers) arrived in England and I remember seeing scores of army lorries driving along the A6 main road with the soldiers sitting in the back. They looked so different from our own soldiers with their smart-looking uniforms and, to my surprise, there were some lorries containing only black men, the first I'd ever seen. Such excitement to this nine-year-old lad! There were to be one and a half million American servicemen posted to the UK during the war.

The American servicemen had a profound influence on our lives. Although we'd been used to watching American cowboy films and their heroic deeds, seeing these ordinary soldiers proved to be a bit of a disappointment. Generally, we were pleased to see them but there were complications and resentments. We had been at war for over two years and were used to going without and making do, but when the American arrived, they had full stomachs and pockets bulging with money.

I'd been told that if you saw an American soldier you had to call out, 'Got any gum, chum?' and they were supposed to throw you a pack of chewing gum, which many Americans always seemed to be chewing; unfortunately, it never worked for me. We had a sweet ration of just two ounces a week which amounted to half a bar of chocolate, so any extra sweets would have been so very welcome to this young lad.

On one occasion, I watched American soldiers playing Craps, which they played by throwing dice against an army steel helmet with pound notes stacked high around each man. I had never imagined anyone could have so much money.

My uncle used to entertain American officers at his home which was opposite their army camp in Leicester. This was situated on the site of what is now the Leicestershire Golf Club. Once, one of the officers looked at his watch and found it had stopped working so he took it off his wrist, dropped it on the floor and crushed it under his foot. This amazed us all because the watch was of so little value to him that he could destroy it so casually, when we would've simply had the watch repaired.

The American servicemen arrived very smartly dressed and full of confidence, with a saunter and a swagger. They came with five times the pay of the British Tommy and with their friendly charm and thick wallets, they conquered the hearts of many British girls. At the end of the war over 60,000 British women married American servicemen and left to live in the United States. Some enjoyed luxurious lives, but others found themselves in dreadful situations. Many returned home the worse for their experience.

At the end of the war, the newsreels in the cinemas showed hundreds of GI brides leaving our shores on ships to start a new life in America but never showed those returning home after being sadly disappointed with the men they'd married.

During his stay in Britain one American soldier wrote home to a friend: "Boy! Alden, so long as there is an England I won't have to worry about being a bachelor." Later in the letter he says: "The air raid shelters sure do come in handy when you are courting a girl," and towards the end of the letter he concludes that it might not be his personal charms that keep the ladies interested, but the chewing gum, candy and nylons that he had available.

One joke told at that time about the American soldiers was concerning a new brand of knickers. It said: 'One Yank and they're off!' Another saying about them was that they were 'over paid, over sexed and over here'. They also had nylon stockings with black seams down the back, welcomed with open arms by many of the girls at the time. They could show a girl a good time with their smooth talking and thick wallets.

The British soldiers were left feeling upset and resentful of the Americans with all their money and attractiveness and the fact they were taking their girlfriends, whilst they were still fighting abroad.

Apart from the jokes, one thing is certain; we couldn't have won the war without the Americans' help and sacrifices, for which we were all very thankful.

In January 1942, my family was evacuated to Tenby because our home had been requisitioned on government orders, to allow the site agent of builders Wimpey to live at our home whilst he supervised the construction of Stoughton airfield.

To me it seemed like an exciting adventure to be leaving home for foreign parts, but my mother did not appreciate being ordered to give up our home so it could be used by a builder, but you had no choice but to accept these impositions. You had to just shrug your shoulders and say, "Well, there's a war on."

The reason we went to Tenby was because it was where my dad was stationed in the Royal Marines at that time, and he managed to find a cottage to rent for our stay in the town.

We left Leicester in the early evening for the overnight train journey to Tenby. The trains during the conflict were packed to bursting point, as members of the armed forces would be travelling from camp to camp, joining the forces or sometimes going on leave, so the trains were much busier than they would have been in peacetime.

Steam trains have a nostalgic appeal these days, but if you had to travel on a long journey during wartime, and at night, it was not a pleasant experience. Many passengers in those days seemed to smoke cigarettes, so the air would be thick with the smell of tobacco as well as the smell of smoke and steam from the engine which would then drift into the carriages, especially if any windows had been left open.

Then you had the problem of finding a seat. If no seats were available you had to stand in the corridor, or if you had a suitcase it would serve as your seat.

I spent a lot of time on the journey looking out of the corridor window and getting smuts of grit from the engine in my eyes. I loved the sound of the wheels on the rails, going 'clickerty click, clickerty clack, clickerty click'. It was a moonlit night when we travelled, so I could make out the shapes of houses and cattle in the fields. Also, the reflection of the moon would shine on the rivers and streams as we passed by.

One of the dangers of travelling by train in those days was that the lights were still illuminated in the carriages, so any stray German aeroplanes could machine-gun the train as it sped along.

We had to change trains at Birmingham and then again at Crewe, which at that time was a major railway junction linking a few important towns, with lines going in six different directions.

On the country to district rail lines, used for short journeys, many of the carriages simply had a walk-through compartment, with doors on either side of the train and no toilets available.

When we arrived in Tenby, tired and dishevelled, my father was waiting for us at the station to take us to our new temporary home.

We stayed in a very small rented cottage at number 14 Lower Frog Street. It had gas lights on the wall, an outside toilet and a tin bath which was brought into the living room and placed in front of the small fireplace and used just once a week. My sisters and I all used the same water, filled with kettles heated on a hob by the side of the small fireplace. Fortunately, I was first in the bath and after a quick wash down, I was sent to bed so my sisters could follow me into the cooling, second-hand water, much to my amusement!

I remember, shortly after our arrival in Tenby in January 1942, seeing a march-past of Royal Marines led by a band which belonged to 15th and 18th Battalion of the Plymouth

Division who were based in Tenby at that time. I looked out for my dad but there were so many Marines in the parade that I couldn't spot him.

I marched alongside the band, by the side of the drummers, for a while, until they turned off to move to another part of town. I imagined I was a soldier as well as the marchers.

One special memory was an early morning visit to Whiffies' Bakery. The owner Mr Wilfred Vaul was known to my father and invited my sister and I to see him baking his bread and cobs. As soon as the cobs left the oven, Mr Vaul cut one open and laid what looked to me like a week's ration of butter into this hot steaming cob. The butter immediately melted throughout the whole of this delicious treat and was eagerly devoured by this hungry young lad.

I went to the local National Council School in Upper Park Road, which was demolished some years ago. My abiding memory was of all the singing we had to do. I remember having to stand on a stool in the classroom, but don't recall the reason. Whether it was for a solo performance of some well-known aria or because I had misbehaved, I do not recall. Probably, it was the latter.

This was the only school, other than infants', at which I avoided being caned, although I did get into one or two scrapes for fighting which incurred a visit to the headmistress for a telling-off. Corporal punishment was an accepted hazard of being a normal boisterous schoolboy in those far-off days.

My sister Mary and I had been logged into the school as unofficial evacuees, so we must have seemed a strange species to the local Welsh natives, and because we'd moved away from the bombing in Leicester we thought we were going to be safe in this town, but we were still to encounter more air-raid warnings in Tenby.

It was quite apparent that I was the only English boy in a Welsh school. At first, they were suspicious of this young lad from the Midlands, which to them was a foreign part of the country, but eventually I was accepted and joined in their many exploits around Tenby.

The head teacher was a Mrs Martha Williams, but my teacher was Miss Griffiths, who was recorded in the school log as frequently being late for class and who claimed she had been working at the local hospital. The log didn't reveal whether Mrs Williams believed her excuse or not, but she was reprimanded just the same.

Discipline was much less strict than the school I'd come from in Leicestershire, and one could escape during certain times of the day to carry out explorations of the area.

The log for the time I was at this school is very revealing and reported poor attendance most of the time that I was there, which partly explains the times my pals and I were bunking off from school. There were so many out-of-the-way places to explore around the town without the possibility of being caught, but on one occasion we were legally given the afternoon off to celebrate St David's Day. Unfortunately, this was also to be counted as our half-term holiday, so on that special day there was no need to be cautious whilst on manoeuvres.

Mrs Williams, recorded the following in the school log for 2nd February 1942:

"Attendance for month is unsatisfactory due to causes other than illness. Prosecution is not being proceeded with because of the war. Several children are working for employers in the town. Attendance for the month is 76%."

On the following day, Mrs Williams reported:

"Miss Davies absent through mothers' illness, Miss Griffiths late presumably through doing hospital work. The absence of teachers and lack of punctuality seriously affects school work."

A further entry revealed:

"Class 10 went on a nature ramble to Waterwynch, returned by sea-shore to study sea-weed. Senior boys spent afternoon gardening."

This description sounds more like a holiday camp than a school!

On one of our illegal afternoon excursions from school, we walked over the cliffs on what appeared to be an empty golf course and my pals proceeded to make a bomb in an empty tin with saltpetre. Even at that time it struck me as being very dangerous. Fortunately, no one was injured.

We had an air raid shelter in the playground, it was a brick-built structure above ground level that didn't seem to be as safe as the ones I'd used in Leicester, which were below ground. These shelters would not have survived a direct hit or even a close bomb blast, but would have protected the children and teachers from small pieces of shrapnel. It didn't occur to me at the time, but a close exploding bomb would have killed all the occupants, including me.

We had quite a few air raid warnings in Tenby in 1942 whilst I was at school. On each occasion, we would hear the warning air-raid sirens sounding their wailing loud and soft song. We would then walk briskly out of the class, in single file, and into the shelter where we were seated on wooden benches, packed like sardines in a tin.

Like the shelters in Leicester, they were dark and smelt of wet concrete and the only light was through small vents high up on the wall.

We stayed in the shelter whilst the German bombers passed overhead until they were out of range, then the siren would sound one continuous wailing noise to announce that the immediate danger was over. This alarm was then repeated on their return journey back to France.

After the defeat of France in 1940, the *Luftwaffe* created an airfield at Cherbourg in northern France which put Liverpool in range of their bombers passing over Tenby on their way to bomb the docks, where ships were unloading supplies from the United States. During these bombing raids, over 4,000 people lost their lives in the Liverpool area.

Apart from the air raids, Tenby was a magical place to live. There were so many places to explore. I have such fond memories of the many attractions of this delightful little town.

One of those was the caves under the cliffs. They were high inside and deep. The floor was scattered with loose rocks and pools of shallow water. At high tide, the cave would be filled with the rolling waves, and not long after the sea had receded, the water would still be trickling down the walls like narrow, snaking arteries.

The whole eerie atmosphere inside the cave warned that this relief from the pounding sea was simply temporary, so whilst you were deep inside, you had a scary feeling in case the sea returned quickly before you could escape.

The caves had a magical atmosphere. If you shouted, your voice would echo back to you so this had to be repeated as many times as was necessary until the enjoyment and curiosity had been satisfied. The caves had an overpowering scent, best described as a mixture of the medicinal delights of the sea.

Our favourite cave was so large, we imagined it could be used as accommodation for a family of giants, had the sea not prevented this.

On another occasion, whilst wandering around Tenby, I spotted an Air-Sea Rescue boat moored against the harbour wall. It had very sleek lines and a sharp high bow, which allowed it to travel quickly through the water to rescue downed airmen from the sea. But, to me as a small boy, what made it special was that it was military and that was such a real treat.

The RAF crew were loading supplies in readiness for their next tour of duty. I stood watching for some time and eventually, when they'd finished, I plucked up the courage to ask if I could look around the boat and, to my surprise and delight, they beckoned me on board.

I jumped on to the deck and they showed me into the cabin where they would treat the rescued airmen for any wounds or exposure. Sometimes, pilots could have been in their small dinghies on the high seas for hours at a time, prior to being recovered. I remember seeing the bright red blankets on each of the two beds. These warm blankets would have been such a comfort to any rescued airman.

The bridge had lots of dials and levers, a compass, steering wheel and a seat for the helmsman. I could imagine the boat speeding through the water and wished I could have had a ride in this beautiful boat, but obviously this was not possible.

These boats had a crew of nine including the Captain and Medical Orderly, and would be on stand-by twenty-four hours a day, for seven days a week.

As Tenby was a tidal harbour with low tide for a few hours every day, the boat would be moored to a buoy outside the harbour to be at the ready for any emergencies, and would only come into the harbour to re-supply, for maintenance or to change crews.

The RAF Marine Branch who operated these boats, saved over 13,000 lives during the Second World War and, whilst undertaking their normal role, even took part in the invasion of France on 6th June 1944.

The U Boat blockade in the Atlantic kept the RAF, based in Pembrokeshire, busily engaged in trying to sink them, hence the need for Air-Sea Rescue.

Two of these high-speed launches operated from Tenby so this one may have been the boat I was allowed on board to look around.

One January night, I wandered through the narrow streets of Tenby heading towards the steep cliffs. The wind howled and the mist swirled in ghostly shapes, as if directed by some unseen force.

It was a particularly dark that night, but as I approached the cliffs' edge the sound of the waves became louder, as if they were angry with the rocks who dared to stand in their way.

I stood at the top of the cliff and listened to the thundering of the waves along with the noise of the wind, and I felt the fine salty sea spray over my face. As I stood there, I was transported into another world. I don't know how long I stood there. It was such a surreal feeling that I lost all sense of time. I was simply in another world.

When I came to my senses, I decided to return to our little cottage. I opened the door and faced an angry mother, and was met with a torrent of abuse.

She held a stick in her hand and proceeded to beat me over the head, in an affectionate show of concern for my well-being!

I was sent to bed without any supper to reflect on the evening's events. The violent abuse was not that unexpected, but the enjoyment of my pleasure at listening to and watching the awesome power of the sea made the evening a wonderful experience, which I still treasure to this day.

By this time in the war, at Tenby, the abnormal became routine with many public buildings and houses being requisitioned for military purposes. Some other properties were required to house homeless evacuees.

The British Restaurant in Tenby supplied 23,324 meals at sixpence a head for the main course, but by the end of the year this had increased to seven pence! A cup of tea cost one 'old' penny.

Before we left Tenby, mines were laid on the beaches to prevent German forces landing so we were denied further escapades in that area.

We left Tenby in August 1942, much to my regret, and returned to Leicester once Stoughton Airfield had been completed and I then returned to Thurnby village school to regale my friends at school with tales of all my adventures.

One day, not long after our return from Tenby, I was called to the classroom in which the headmaster Mr Palmer taught and was made to stand in front of the class until he was ready to talk to me, not knowing why I'd been summoned. After a few minutes, he came over to me and informed me I was to be punished, because of a complaint my mother had made to him about my conduct.

He ordered me to hold out my hand and revealed a cane he had been holding by his side. He raised the cane high above his shoulder. I closed my eyes and heard the swish of the cane descending and then felt a burning, searing pain go through my hand and up into my arm. He repeated this once more on the same hand and then ordered me to hold out my left hand and, once again, started the punishment with the same vigorous determination, *"Do as you're told in future,"* he ordered. *"Now go back to your class."*

On my return to my classroom, holding back the tears, I thought of the loathing I felt for the person who'd ordered this cruel punishment, for what had been such a minor infringement as meeting a friend of whom my mother disapproved.

My relationship with my mother never recovered after this incident, although I had no option but to accept much of her hospitality as was necessary after this and other abuses I'd suffered from her.

On one occasion at the village school we had a visit from the dentist, who appeared in a long white coat. He was thin and gaunt, which gave the impression of him being an undertaker rather than a caring professional dentist. He was a fearsome character and with his blunt manner bade me 'Sit there'. The seat was a temporary structure which looked more like a barber's chair. He then poked around with his metal probe in my mouth and to my absolute relief could not find a tooth which required his attention.

The most frightening item was the drill which stood on a large black stand and was operated by a foot treadle. Presumably this would be controlled at whatever speed this man deemed appropriate for the torture of young boys and girls. This experience gave me a permanent fear of dentists.

Another frequent occurrence at school was a visit from the nit nurse, who used a very fine-tooth comb to search for fleas! Fortunately, I remained flea-free!

We were given a meal at mid-day at school and the most memorable feast for me was the cheesy potatoes. I can still taste them to this day!

In August of '42, my dad left Tenby and commenced Royal Marine Commando training at Lympstone in Devon, followed by six weeks' arduous battle training at the remote training base at Achnacarry in Scotland. Live ammunition and explosives were used close to the trainees to give them a sense of what battle conditions were really like, and it was said by many of these men that it really helped them when they experienced actual battle.

My father was still attached to the battalion in Tenby until he completed his commando training. In the event of him failing to complete the course, he would have been RTU'd (Returned to Unit).

He completed the course and was awarded his green beret in October 1942. He must have been one of the oldest men ever to have passed the course. Many men younger than him had failed the rigorous tests to become Commandos. He was 36 years old, considered quite elderly in those days.

Once he'd qualified as a Commando, it was accepted that he'd volunteered for hazardous service so that his chances of survival would be much reduced. However, this enabled him to join an elite fighting unit, rather than possibly being stuck in an office behind the front lines during the conflict.

On 19th August, a task force set out for the coast of France, aiming for the town of Dieppe with a large force of Canadian and Essex Scottish troops, who were to secure a bridgehead in the town to allow the 31 men of 40 Royal Marine Commando, involved in a 'pinch' raid, to steal a three wheeled Enigma machine, together with codes and ciphers from the German Naval Headquarters based in the Hotel Moderne just a short distance from the harbour.

The Commando raid was led by Lieutenant 'Peter' Huntington-Whitely, RM, and Sergeant Johnny Kruthhoffer, who was to give me his first-hand account of his involvement in this raid when I spoke to him after the war. He explained in minute detail his whole experience, as if he'd just returned! Johnny and my father joined 30 Commando from its inception after the Dieppe raid until the end of the war and became good friends.

He told me that my father always kept up with his younger colleagues and never used his age to refuse any task. He related a tale of when they were in Algeria together and they'd used a heavily armed jeep to ride along the coast to try to find a source of beer, but without any success.

In Dieppe, HMS Locus, with the Commandos on board, was to sail into the harbour and dock by the harbour wall to allow the Commandos to swiftly attack the hotel and secure the intelligence after the harbour had been secured by the

Canadian troops. However, everything that could go wrong went wrong.

The ships were supposed to arrive before dawn but, thanks to the Royal Navy, they arrived late, and in daylight, thereby losing the element of surprise. The German forces were soon alerted and opened-up with a huge shelling barrage and machine-gun fire, preventing the Canadian troops from securing a bridgehead in the town.

Disaster was to follow. Almost 1000 Canadians were killed in the attack, 2,400 were injured and 2,000 more were taken prisoner to spend the remainder of the war in captivity.

Although the bridgehead in the harbour was not secured, HMS Locus still attempted to steer into the town but was struck by a shell and had to withdraw. They then attempted to land a little further down the coast, but were again prevented from doing so by heavy gunfire, and therefore had to return to the UK.

Offshore, a fast destroyer had waited with James Bond author, Ian Fleming, on board with the intention of collecting the intelligence and returning it to Bletchley Park for analysis, but he had to return empty handed.

In September of 1942, just a month after the Dieppe raid, the creation of 30 Commando was officially revealed.

Commander Ian Fleming, who'd been involved in organising the Commando assault on Dieppe, received the agreement of the Director of Naval Intelligence and Lord Louis Mountbatten to form a Special Intelligence Gathering Unit, comprised mostly of Royal Marine Commandos, used for assault and collection of intelligence, together with an assortment of men from the Royal Navy and a small section from the Army.

Various scientists and other specialists became part of this unit being required to evaluate the usefulness of captured equipment, documents, codes and ciphers for later analysis by military experts or passed to Bletchley Park for investigation.

Its first name was 30 RN Commando (Special Engineering Unit), and was later being renamed 30 Assault

Unit. They were designated as 'Authorised Looters' to carry out 'Pinch' raids.

The unit was generally disliked by military commanders because 30 Commando was totally independent and carried out covert infiltrations into enemy territory without their knowledge or authority to enable the capture of all forms of military equipment, documents, codes or important German personnel. This freedom from authority did not endear them to higher command, but it was vitally important to maintain the utmost secrecy to enable them to obtain much valuable intelligence without interference.

The unit's motto was 'Attain by Surprise'. Most of the operations were to be behind enemy lines; the men being infiltrated by land, parachute or from Naval assault craft. Ian Fleming referred to his men as 'Red Indians'.

Following the unsuccessful raid on Dieppe, Huntington-Whitely commenced his selection for 30 Commando of men whom he considered the most suitable candidates for what was described as 'very hazardous missions' after exhaustive interviews.

Firstly, he chose a few of the colleagues who'd been with him on the Dieppe raid, and then proceeded to interview other volunteers. The interview was carried out on a very friendly and informal basis and my father was asked to sit down, which was unusual when being interviewed by an officer. He then asked him a few general questions about himself and his civilian life, family and interests. Finally, he then told him that he should understand that this was a very hazardous service, and he should think carefully before deciding if he was still willing to volunteer for this unit.

A few days after the interview my father was told he'd been selected and accepted the invitation to join this unit. Only those who Captain Huntington-Whitely considered to be made of the 'right stuff' were to be chosen. My father was one of the first Royal Marines to join this elite Commando unit. Amongst his other attributes was his ability to speak fluent German.

The recruits to this newly formed unit soon began specialist training in the 'dark-art' of intelligence gathering, many of these techniques have remained a secret to this day, other than to Special Forces.

Special Forces were paid an extra six shilling and eight pence extra, per day, over and above normal soldiers' pay. He was expected to pay for his lodgings out of this extra money, which cost about thirty shillings a week, so he was left with sufficient cash to buy whatever he chose, including beer at a shilling a pint. This extra pay allowed for what may have turned out to be a somewhat reduced lifespan.

During the war I was to meet many of the men of 30 Commando, later renamed 30 Assault Unit, and it always seemed to me that they, rightly, had this air of superiority through having been chosen to become a member of one of the most elite fighting units within the British Armed Forces.

I met these men before and after they'd been involved in very dangerous missions behind enemy lines, but they appeared to have a scornful disregard for their own safety. I think they simply had a thirst for dangerous situations. I believe they simply craved the excitement of danger.

When you consider why anyone would be foolhardy enough to drive through enemy lines in an open jeep, wearing a British Army uniform, whilst wearing the same shape of steel helmets (Turtle-shaped) worn by their own Special Forces, displaying heavy-calibre cannon machine guns and not expect to be killed or captured, is difficult to understand. But this is how they penetrated the enemy lines on many occasions with minimal losses.

Strangely, the helmets worn by men of 30 AU were very similar, if not identical, to those worn by men of the Brandenburg Regiment; a German intelligence-gathering unit with the same objectives as 30 AU. This German military unit may have been the model copied by Ian Fleming, as this had been created long before 30 AU.

I imagine the German Army could not believe that anyone could be foolish enough to simply drive through their lines in such an audacious way, so maybe they thought it was some of their own Brandenburg men returning from a mission.

Considering the bravery of these men, which in normal wartime circumstances would have earned them the highest military bravery awards, in fact few of them were ever awarded gallantry medals whilst serving with 30 AU, simply because most their missions were so secret, which many have remained to this day.

The Royal Marines of 30 Assault Unit had what was known as the 'black book' with prospective objectives to steal from behind enemy lines and to obtain various military intelligence before it could be destroyed or removed by the German defences.

Their spoils would then be returned to Naval Intelligence at the Admiralty in London and Bletchley Park to be examined by the scientists and specialists. Some of their notable successes were the capture of important military personnel and scientists, to be revealed later in this story.

The best known apparent fiction in Ian Fleming's James Bond books, *'A Licence to Kill'* was a direct reference to an actual order signed by Ian Fleming to officers of the unit which read: 'The necessity for avoiding or eliminating witnesses to successful action is to be emphasised.'

Another warning from Ian Fleming to the men of his unit was made quite clear, that they would face jail or execution if they revealed any details about the work of the unit.

Later in the story, I will relate two actual incidents of this becoming a reality, although these are most likely not the only ones that occurred. The rules of war were generally ignored in the pursuit of obtaining enemy secrets, and anyone obstructing this pursuit would be the worse for their refusal.

An indication of their reputation amongst the American forces is the comment of one famous American Commander, General Douglas MacArthur, who referred to the men of this unit as 'a bunch of Limey gangsters' and you would have to admit that this reputation was not too far from the truth.

Since these men were risking their own lives to achieve their objectives, they did whatever it took to achieve them, which on occasions was in breach of the Geneva Convention. I believe this is one of the reasons why the intimate story of this unit was never allowed to become public knowledge.

The unit's operational role was quite varied: Apart from their main function of penetrating through the enemy lines ahead of advancing Allied Forces to carry out various specified objectives, they also could be used as a strike force for the capture of bridges prior to the arrival of the main assault force, although this was only done in exceptional circumstances, because of the risk of losing such highly trained specialists. After each mission, they would return to their headquarters awaiting their next assignment.

They were also involved in sabotage with the use of explosives for which they'd received extensive training from a convicted safe breaker and cat burglar, Johnny Ramensky; a Scotsman of Lithuanian descent, he had been released from Peterhead prison and given a full pardon so he could pass on professional expertise to men of the unit. My father told me he'd gained enough knowledge to be able to make a good living from such an enterprise, but declined the opportunity.

Johnny must have been quite a character as he'd escaped on two occasions from jail in Glasgow. After the war ended, he resumed his normal activities and was incarcerated once more!

Another task was to capture important enemy personnel who would sometimes have to be persuaded, in a not-too-courteous manner, to reveal important information.

Although the activities of the unit were top secret, some of the successes became known after the war ended, such as the recovery of a turbine-driven torpedo, which was discovered too late in the war to be of very much use, although the technology was no doubt useful for future development. In November 1942, whilst the unit was preparing and training for the tasks ahead at their headquarters at Cold Morham Farm, near Amersham, Bucks, the Admiralty decided they should take part in the assault on North Africa.

This is the unlikely looking headquarters of 30 Assault Unit at Cold Morham farmhouse in the remote countryside near Amersham, Bucks, where clandestine training operations could be carried out in secret.

This became my father's first military assault, Operation Torch, which took place on 8th November 1942.

This small number of men landed to the west of Algiers at Sidi Ferruch. He was on HMS Malcolm which was heavily shelled and badly damaged.

My father and his colleagues had moved from one side of the ship to the other to prepare for landing and where they'd been standing a shell struck the ship, killing and injuring some American soldiers who were to be part of this assault; a lucky move which saved their lives.

They eventually got ashore and following the detailed maps and photographs they'd been given of the area on the outskirts of the city, they located the Italian naval headquarters and captured all the battle orders for the German and Italian fleets and gathered current code books and other useful documents, together with a four-wheel Enigma encoding machine. The following day all this material, amounting to two tons in weight, was returned to the UK in a fast destroyer.

My father told me they spent a couple of weeks searching for other material without much success, then they returned to the UK to their headquarters at Cold Morham by Dakota aircraft which he described as very noisy and uncomfortable for such a long flight.

The story I relate of 30 Assault Unit is from actual conversations with my father, Ron Muddimer, and his Royal Marine Commando colleagues, Kenneth McGregor, Johnny Kruthhoffer, Peter Jemmett and Sid Ryder, as well as from official sources, so it's not always necessary to mention who said what in this narrative in every instance, but simply to acknowledge their involvement in this secret war, and the bravery of these men who put their lives in extreme danger to assist the Allies in winning the war on the basis of valuable intelligence.

Although I was much too young to take part in their activities, I was closely involved with members of this brave band of brothers so this was a very important part of my young life.

As we reached the end of 1942, we all became more confident of a successful outcome to the war, especially after our victory at the battle of El Alamein. Also, the threat of invasion had diminished.

It's difficult to describe the excitement and joy that this successful battle had on us all. It was probably the turning point of the war.
General Montgomery was hailed as a hero for defeating this proud and thus-far successful German Army.

The Royal Navy had blockaded access ports which prevented the Germans re-supplying their army which greatly assisted our army.

The cinemas all showed the start of the battle, with a huge night-time artillery bombardment which gave a big boost to our morale.

Whenever I was out of school term, I would spend many hours out in the countryside away from my very unpleasant 'home' in what seemed like permanent hot and sunny weather in those treasured days.

The countryside was so quiet and peaceful then. As I walked over fields and along dark tree-lined lanes, I could hear the merry song of the skylark, who fluttered above me, chattering and singing his delightful song to whomever wished to listen, as if to declare: 'I'm the happiest bird in the sky.'

I could walk for miles without meeting a soul. It was the solitude that gave me so much pleasure, and taking in all the beautiful sights and sounds of the countryside, not wanting the day to ever end or to return to the place where I lived.

If it rained whilst I was at home, I would sit at the criss-crossed taped-up windows looking out and waiting for the rain to stop, so I could resume my adventures outdoors. Our windows were taped up with a clear adhesive tape to prevent broken glass from splintering and injuring those in the house in the event of a close bomb blast.

As my dad was in the Special Forces during the war, he was never stationed in barracks other than for his Royal Marine Commando training in Devon and battle training in the mountains of Scotland, but was always billeted out in private homes.

We followed my father around to the various towns to which he had been posted, whilst he trained for various specialist tasks. We spent some time in Exmouth whilst my father was at Lympstone doing his initial Royal Marine Commando training, and I used to play with some evacuees who had been sent down from the East End of London.

Their hosts were paid to look after them, but some of these kids told me they were very badly treated, so it must have been dreadful not only being parted from their own families but being abused as well. I'm sure not all evacuees were treated so badly, as I heard other stories that some children were treated kindly as part of the families with whom they lived.

On the night of 3/4th October 1942, twelve men of the Special Operations Executive's Small-Scale Raiding Force and No 12 Commando landed on the German occupied island of Sark in the Channel Islands with the intention of capturing prisoners for offensive intelligence.

They broke into the house of a local lady, Mrs Pittard, who told the men that there were 20 German soldiers based in the nearby Dixcart Hotel. She also told them that people had been deported to Germany for slave labour as a first indication of war crimes.

The Commandos captured five of the soldiers, and to prevent them from running away, they tied their hands behind their backs and made them take off their braces and belts and loosen their flies, so they had to hold up their trousers to prevent them from running away.

They left the five under guard of one of the Commandos to go to look for the remaining 15 soldiers, but one of the captured Germans shouted out a warning to the others, upon which he was shot dead by the guard.

Now alerted, the other Germans opened fire causing the Commandos to withdraw with only one prisoner as the other four had managed to escape during the fire-fight.

Once delivered to the UK, this one remaining captured prisoner did provide useful information after being interrogated.

When Hitler learned of this incident a few days later, he issued the infamous 'Commando Order' which effectively was a death sentence on any Commandos captured in future with the instruction that this information was not to fall into the hands of the Allies, with it being in breach of the Geneva Convention for the conduct of war.

His order read as follows:

"From now on, all men operating against German troops in so-called Commando raids in Europe or in Africa are to be annihilated to the last man. Even if these individuals, on discovery, make obvious their intention of giving themselves up as prisoners. No pardon is on any account to be given. On this matter, a report is to be made in each case to headquarters for the information of Higher Command."

A few weeks later in early December, a Royal Marine Commando, Special Boat Squadron raid, Operation Frankton, took place with the intention of sinking German ships in Bordeaux harbour. Five two-men canoes set out after leaving the submarine HMS Tuna, but only two boats survived the journey up the river Gironde to plant limpet mines on five ships which were badly damaged.

Only two men escaped and returned to England. This raid was to become known as 'The Cockleshell Heroes' after the film of this name.

It was only a few weeks later, following Hitler's 'Commando Order', that six of the 'Cockleshell Heroes' who'd been captured were summarily shot dead after being tortured.

It was not long after this terrible incident that the name of my dad's unit was changed from 30 Commando to 30 Assault Unit, because of intelligence received of these killings and Hitler's 'Commando Order'.

During this period of the war, there was the frequent sight in the sky of the barrage balloon, close to large towns and cities, a large dark-grey balloon, which had three tail fins. It was secured to the ground by a steel cable, the intention being that German planes would fly into the cable in the dark and bring them crashing down to earth. I never heard of this being successful, but they looked nice in the sky.

Whilst travelling on a bus to school, I overheard two elderly gentlemen talking and one of them was relating what had happened to a friend of his who had been sentenced to receive six strokes of the birch for some serious misdemeanour and how he'd lived in fear for the rest of his life of a repeat of this barbaric punishment. In those days severe punishments were considered to be necessary. Fortunately, we've moved on from those cruel days.

My most enjoyable pleasure during the 1940s was visiting the cinema, where I could temporarily forget the unpleasant aspects of my life and be lost in a world of fantasy and imagination. I mostly preferred the Certificate A films, which required a youngster to be accompanied by an adult, so I would wait outside the cinema for a suitable candidate and ask him or her if they would accompany me to the desk. I would pass my money over and after they'd obtained the tickets, I'd leave and go to sit somewhere else. On occasions, I would sit through two sittings of the same film as the screenings continued in those days, one after the other, without the cinema emptying.

1943

On one of my adventures with my pals, we passed along the road by the side of Stoughton aerodrome where we noticed a gap in the hedge and on the other side was a Stirling bomber, so we downed our bikes and pushed through the hole and stood by the plane. There was a step ladder leading to the entrance, so we gingerly climbed step by step until we reached it and looked down the body of the plane. There were empty gun cartridges all over the floor. We could see right up to the flight deck, then we became scared that it might take off and take us to Germany, so we climbed down and quickly cycled off down the road towards Thurnby in case we had been seen.

The Stoughton base was known as RAF Leicester East and occupied by 190 Squadron RAF. The Short Stirling bomber was used for towing gliders and supply drops and these were engaged on D-Day when they made one sortie dropping airborne troops, along with other similar planes towing gliders. At Arnhem, they made 53 supply drops and 18 aircrafts were lost.

On our return home from Stoughton, we stopped for a chat and I climbed onto a high five-bar fence to rest, but when I reached the top, I fell straight into an adjacent blackberry bush. The thorns lacerated my hands quite badly, so we had to rush home for treatment. The cure was to be worse than the actual injury because iodine was applied, which was the recommended antiseptic remedy for cuts and scratches available at that time. The pain of this application was excruciating. I still bear the scars from this misadventure on my hands and arms to this day!

One of our favourite enterprises was to play in the sand pit in Thurnby where there was an old Bren-gun-carrier, a small machine-gun carrying tank, which I imagine had got stuck half way down a steep slope, or maybe had been used by the Home Guard as practice. In any event, it gave my pals and me many hours of war games, shooting many German soldiers in the process.

Hedges and dry ditches were always useful for building dens, to create a hide so we could not be seen by any strangers. These would have a flat area for sitting and discussing important plans for our future activities and would be built with any loose branches for camouflage.

I'd always been fond of cats until one particular day, when a ginger-coloured, 'tiger-looking' cat with a long bushy tail appeared in our garden. So, thinking it may need feeding, I went into our kitchen to get a saucer of milk and laid it in front of this feral beast, whereupon it dived at my leg and sank its teeth into my shin. To this day, I can still see its teeth which looked more like fangs. Not surprisingly, after this assault, I have disliked this species of animal ever since.

In the winter-time when the snow and ice often seemed to appear in the new year, we would create an ice slide on a down slope in the school playground. The boys would slide on the snow and, quite quickly, it would be turned into an icy slide. You took a run over the snow and then slid down the slope at a fast speed. It was such great excitement for a young boy. No health and safety in those days! So if you fell over, you just got up, dusted yourself down and went back for another go.

The girls would play 'Hopscotch' in the playground. They had a row of single and double chalk-drawn squares into which they would hop and jump from the single to the double square. I could never quite see the point, but then I suppose they thought some of the boys' games were pointless too.

Skipping was another pastime enjoyed by the girls and sometimes they would have two girls holding either end of the rope, and up to three girls would skip in the middle with each revolution. It always looked very clever to me. Probably something the boys couldn't do as well as the girls.

'Whip and Top' was something else we enjoyed. You had a thin leather whip on the end of a stick and a top shaped like a screw-in bottle top, and another one called a carrot which, for obvious reasons, was shaped just like a thick, short, stubby carrot. The bottle top type was easy to get spinning and you kept whipping it to make it turn faster and faster. The carrot-top was much more difficult to get spinning, and I never managed the task.

'Snobs' was another game. You had four or five square snobs, the size of dice and made of some hard material which seemed like rock. You would then place the required number in the palm of your hand and throw them into the air and try to get them to land on the back of your hand. The more you could catch there, the greater chance you had of winning.

I don't know if yoyos are still made, but it was two discs joined together with an open centre, which had a string attached. You wound the string around the middle and then released it by throwing the disc towards the ground whilst still holding the end of the string. Then you could make it fall and rise by pulling the string each time it fell, which made it return to your hand. The longer you could continue this motion, the better the enjoyment.

'Leapfrog' was another pastime where you would bend over with your back to the one or more children behind you who would vault over you and then they would bend over to allow more children to leap over them. You could then have a continuous line of bending and leaping children.

Single-decker buses used to have an emergency exit at the rear with a long handle to release the door for a quick exit. On one occasion, I was returning from school when a handicapped youngster pulled this handle and fell out of the bus and onto the road whilst the bus was still moving. I believe the poor lad did not survive his fall.

During this time in the forties, disabled people were not treated with very much sympathy, other than by their own families, of course. Attitudes nowadays have changed to the extent that the disabled are mostly treated with sympathy and consideration.

I believe it was in 1943 that my father was home on leave. He had gone to a local pub with my mother and returned home with two RAF fighter pilots who'd fought in the Battle of Britain. I was in absolute awe to meet these two men. Try to imagine the excitement of this ten-year-old lad at meeting these two heroes. Of course, I'd read all about the exploits of this famous battle and how these brave men of the Royal Air Force had saved us from certain invasion.

Defeat against Germany would have resulted in us being under the control of Hitler and his Gestapo Secret Police which we all feared.

One of the pilots was decorated with the DSO (Distinguished Service Order) and the DFC (Distinguished Flying Cross) and bar, which meant he had won this same medal on two separate occasions. The other had won the DFC. These are the very same men described by Winston Churchill with the words: *"Never was so much owed by so many to so few,"* and I was in the company of these brave heroes. I asked a few questions about their medals but refrained from asking how they had won them. It was something you didn't ask those who'd fought in battle in those days.

These men had fought in the skies above Southern England against the German fighters, who were sent to protect their bombers, and whose intention was to destroy our air fields and air force in preparation for invading England.

It is impossible to describe in words my feelings of wonder and excitement at meeting these two airmen. To me they were simply 'god like'. Even to a ten-year-old they looked young. Some of these men were no more than 18 years of age and fighting for their lives in the air. Taking off and flying in many sorties every day for weeks on end, not knowing if they would survive to the next. Their fight for our freedom was an act of the utmost bravery.

Every Christmas day we'd wait for King George to make his annual speech on the radio. We would wait anxiously for him to commence as he suffered with a bad stammer. We all hoped he would manage to get through his message without stopping altogether, so it was a great relief when he finished without a long pause. We had a great respect for the King and Queen during the war because they stayed in London during the Blitz to be with all their subjects. They would often visit bombed out families to show their support. Some very famous people left the country to live in Canada during the war to avoid any danger. We considered them to be cowards.

During this year, preparations for D-Day became intense. You could often see the American airborne soldiers dropping from aircraft with their silk camouflaged canopies, a lovely sight for a young boy to witness.

Also, you could see Stirling bombers from Stoughton airfield towing gliders. Sometimes a bomber would practise towing two gliders at the same time. On one occasion, a glider missed its allocated landing site and landed in a field close to our home, so this could be used for our manoeuvres until the military removed it back to Stoughton.

On 10th July, my dad took part in the invasion of Sicily and remained there until October, the unit having completed their intelligence gathering tasks.

When my father was fighting abroad, we were never permitted to know where he was, so we addressed our air-mail letters to a British Forces Post Office (BFPO) with simply a number.

The air-mail letters we used were just one sheet of very thin paper which had to be folded and glued on one edge, once the letter was written.

By 1943, we'd all become accustomed to coping with the effects of tragedy and death in wartime Britain, and my father more so than myself as a mere civilian, because of the many times he'd fought against the enemy, but other than normal conflict there was one incident which was to have a profound and lasting effect on him.

My father's unit was part of the invasion of Sicily, being landed by assault landing craft on the beaches close to the town of Syracuse, with the objective of collecting intelligence in the port of this town.

So that a bridge-head could be established on the coast, it was intended that a glider force with soldiers of the Air

Landing Brigade would land some miles inland to allow the assault from the beaches to succeed quickly and with minimal casualties.

On 9th July, the towing planes, piloted by American airmen who'd never faced battle conditions before, approached the coast and faced a barrage of anti-aircraft fire from the Italian forces. Rather than continue inland to release the gliders, they panicked and, in an act of cowardice, released many of the gliders before reaching the coast. As a result, 65 gliders fell into the sea, costing the lives of 252 British soldiers who'd drowned without any hope of being rescued.

Over the next few weeks the bodies of these drowned soldiers were being washed up on the beach almost every day and my father had the task, along with his colleagues, of recovering their bodies. Although he told me about this tragedy after the war had ended, it was clear he still suffered from this terrible experience and never forgave the American pilots for their cowardly act.

When my father returned from Sicily, he brought back a large bag of almonds for me. Having set up camp in an almond grove, he'd had a ready supply of these treats which he'd cracked open from their shells in his spare time. Not having ever tasted these nuts before, it didn't take long before these delicious contents were devoured.

By the beginning of 1943, village life had returned to what had existed for many years previously, other than for shortages of almost every kind of food and domestic articles, and the inconvenience still of black-outs.

In our village we still had the cobbler to mend our shoes, as these had to be made to last much longer than in previous years. His shop always had the distinctive smell of leather.

I was fascinated to watch the cobbler at work. Firstly, he would place the shoe over a steel last, then strip off the existing leather sole and cut a piece of leather to approximately fit around the shoe from a large hide. He'd place this on top and then nail around the sole into the base of the shoe. He held a quantity of nails between his lips and withdrew each nail as required. Bang, bang, bang. In quick succession, he'd nail around the sole, and when that was done, he'd trim around the sole with a very sharp knife to make a neat edge.

He must have repaired hundreds of shoes in his time as a cobbler, which allowed him to expertly mend footwear so quickly.

He held a stock of 'Phillips' steel toe-caps, which could be nailed into your heels and toes to extend the life of shoes, before the soles and heels needed replacing. He also stocked various coloured dyes to restore scuffed leather to its original hue.

Our church, St Luke's in Thurnby, was still an important part of village life, with Sunday services held in the morning and evening. The vicar was a well-respected gentleman who treated his parish as his responsibility and would visit the elderly in their homes to offer them 'eternal life', as he believed.

He also visited the sick and those in need of comfort from the death of loved ones.

The congregation in church consisted mostly of elderly men and women, with a few youngsters, as so many men and women had been conscripted into the forces and were working to aid the war effort.

I was a member of the choir, although I've never considered myself as religious, or much of a singer, but probably my voice would be drowned out by those who could sing in tune.

The only time I could be heard above all the others in the choir was when I sang 'Onward Christian Soldiers' when all the members of the choir would turn and give me a look of reproach.

My favourite time of the year in church was the 'Harvest Festival', when the whole church would be decorated with a vast selection of fruit, vegetables and flowers which, after the services had finished, would be distributed to the village elderly and poor. In those days, the poor were really poor, but they were often helped by the better-off people of the village.

If you needed to telephone someone a long distance from your home, you dialled 100 to speak to the operator, and where we lived, the exchange was situated in the village of Thurnby.

The exchange was manned by the Fielding family who would know almost everyone who called. You would give them the number you wanted and they would then get connected to the next large town and continue through various connections until they reached the destination you required. This could have gone through many exchanges before you spoke to the person you wanted. After you'd finished your conversation, and your receiver was replaced, each exchange in turn would hear a buzzing noise so they could disconnect the call.

The Rose and Crown was our village public house. When my father was on leave from the forces he would sometimes take me along. I would wait outside to be provided with a bottle of lemonade, with a straw and if very lucky, I'd get a crusty cheese cob which would be delivered through the 'off sales' window by the landlord. During the war, children weren't allowed in pubs.

The village postman was always eagerly awaited by those wanting to hear from loved ones serving in the forces overseas, but the telegram delivery boy, on his red bicycle, with his smart uniform and his peaked cap was a feared sight, as he was the one who delivered telegrams with news of the death of someone's husband, son or loved one.

I imagine every village in the land had its characters and Thurnby was no exception. The local policeman PC 'Copper' Waldron, rode about on his 'sit-up-and-beg' bicycle in a most authoritative manner to demonstrate his position as administrator of law and order.

I don't think he had very much to contend with, although the village had one or two burglaries in the war, but these were investigated by two detectives from Leicester who arrived in gabardine raincoats and trilby hats, but no prosecutions ever followed.

There was one cripple in our village with a club foot and another young man who was mentally disabled. At a time when village people rarely moved from their own area, interbreeding with close relatives was quite common, and this sometimes resulted in their offspring being mentally disabled. Many English villages suffered from this during this period and from earlier times.

My father told me of an occasion in 1943 when he and some other men from his elite special forces unit were tasked with protecting Winston Churchill whilst he was residing at the Admiralty Citadel, a building erected to protect government ministers in the event of a German invasion. He never told me why this was necessary but I believe it must have been because intelligence had been received of a threat to Churchill's life.

Mr Churchill was normally protected by a dedicated police detail, so it may explain how serious the threat was being taken at that time. My father never told me if he'd met Winston Churchill, but I would imagine he must have if he'd been detailed to protect him.

1944

It must have been during the school term, but my two sisters, my mother and I stayed in lodgings in Littlehampton just before the D-Day invasion on 6th June. Most of the streets were lined with all kinds of army vehicles, lorries, tanks and ambulances which were painted with a big red cross on each side.

All the military vehicles were painted with three thick black and white lines on their bonnets, with planes likewise painted on their wings and fuselage so they could be distinguished easily during the assault on Europe.

None of the vehicles of 30 Assault Unit were painted with these distinguishing lines, but simply a white star enclosed in a white circle, in the hope of confusing the Germans into thinking they were part of their own forces.

During this pre-invasion period, visitors to the area of the south coast needed a special pass to visit or stay for any length of time, so my father had to obtain a pass for our stay in Littlehampton.

Except for Special Forces, other soldiers were not even allowed out of their camps for the few days before 6th June. Security was at its most severe level to prevent giving any clue to the Germans of the forthcoming assault.

'A Licence to Kill' became a reality in Littlehampton after one of the Marine Commandos was heard by Navy spies talking to civilians in a local pub about the secret work of 30 Assault Unit, in breach of strict official orders.

This photograph of 30 Assault Unit HQ Troop was taken shortly before the D-Day landings. The Marine standing on the left-hand side, Harry Porter, did not survive the battle. My dad is seated on the left of the picture with Captain Sid Ryder, his boss, sitting next to him.

Breach of these orders did not officially carry the death penalty, but the men had been warned by Ian Fleming that they could face jail or execution if they revealed the secret work of the unit to outsiders. When I spoke to one of my father's colleagues after the war, he told me he was in no doubt that this man was taken away and shot. He couldn't be 'returned to unit' or jailed as he was likely to reveal his knowledge to other people, so the Commanding Officer made the decision to execute him as it was so close to D-Day. This man was never seen or heard of again.

I was probably in Littlehampton when this incident occurred, as it happened shortly before D-Day, although I didn't learn of it until after the war had ended.

After this event, the Commanding Officer warned all the men of the seriousness of giving away secrets, which could put the work of the unit at risk if the enemy were to discover their covert work. He claimed this marine had been jailed and complained that all the extensive training given to this man had been wasted.

The fact that the Commanding Officer claimed that this marine had been jailed, simply isn't credible because he wouldn't have been jailed without a 'Court Marshall', and this did not occur because that would have then revealed the secret work of the unit to outsiders. So, the claim of his colleagues that he was executed becomes more credible during this extremely sensitive time just prior to the invasion of Europe.

This was a very exciting time for us all as it could lead to the end of the war.

Once the invasion had begun, we were all very worried in case the invasion forces were driven back into the sea, but after a few days, it was clear that a secure bridge-head had been secured.

Whilst the preparations were in full swing prior to the D-Day landings, my own life continued as normal; so in the school holidays I would visit Humberstone Park with my pals, which was opposite the tram terminus. It seemed like a vast area to a small lad. It had a boating lake with paddle boats which were operated by handles turning the paddles independently to manoeuvre from side to side, forwards or backwards, or around in circles. After these exertions, if you had sufficient funds, you could buy an ice cream from the cafe.

The park had a superintendent, who was given an unpleasant name because of his fearsome reputation among small boys, so it was in your best interests to keep a safe distance and not to upset him.

When I was eleven, I was allowed to go swimming by myself at the Lido outdoor swimming pool, which stretched through from Uppingham Road on one side to Scraptoft Lane on the other, a distance of a few hundred yards.

I learnt to swim by watching how other people swam and, little by little, I could swim a few yards up to the edge of the baths. Then in time I would increase the distance, a few strokes at a time, until I could swim a longer distance.

It had a very high diving board and it wasn't long before I would stand at the top, and when I'd plucked up sufficient courage, I would leap off and hope I was still upright when I hit the water. The worst that could happen was that you had what was called a 'belly flop', when you landed on your front or back, which caused a very unpleasant pain for some while afterwards, and in an extreme fall could have caused death!

They had a lovely grassed area where people used to sunbathe and chat with their friends. In the changing-room they had a Brylcreem hair-cream dispenser, and for a couple of pennies, you could squeeze a couple of shots to plaster your hair so you looked just like the adverts of the famous cricketer Denis Compton.

The swimming pool had two sessions, morning and afternoon, and after the first session they would empty the whole area and close the pool. Later, it would re-open for the afternoon session when you would be required to pay again. One of my friends used to hide until the second group of swimmers entered, and then would reappear to avoid having to pay for a second session. He wishes to remain anonymous!

I travelled to school in Leicester by tram. The sound of the trams could have been an orchestra playing a symphony of unnatural sounds, to the delight of the passengers. At each bend in the road, the wheels would squeal out in pain; on the straight, they would howl with pleasure at being let off the leash, and all through the journey, the whole tram would be shaking and rattling with its own unique sounds of motion whilst running along its steel roadway.

At every stop, when a passenger wished to get off the tram, the conductor would pull an overhead cord to ring the bell to warn the driver to stop, and pull the cord again to tell the driver to move off.

The conductor would be calling 'Tickets please' to those who hadn't paid and 'Move down the tram' when it was standing-room only.

He would have to climb the stairs to sell his tickets to passengers on the upper floor and would be clattering up the metal stairs and down again, to add to all the other familiar sounds.

The driver sat in his cab at the front of the tram which was open at one side whatever the weather. The tram could be driven from either end so when it reached the end of the line, he would get off and move the long pole on the roof which had a wheel at the end and which slotted onto an overhead electric cable, so he could drive the tram back in the opposite direction.

Many trams had wooden seats with reversible back rests, which could be turned in the opposite direction, so you would be facing forwards on the return journey. At the terminus, the conductor would move along the tram clattering each seat into its new position.

The driver had a turning handle to start the tram moving which was accompanied by the whirring noise as the tram sped away. When the driver applied the brake this also had its own familiar clatter. Many tram drivers quite rightly seemed to have an air of importance, being responsible for their passengers, and their own vehicle.

Qh 1196

1D

Rodley Terminus		Hough Lane
Pudsey Terminus		Brown Cow
Wesley Terminus		Bramley Station
Stanningley		Tow...
BrownCow or Broad Lane		Moorfield Road
Hough Ln. or Bramley Station		Branch Road
Moorfield Road		Queen Street
Branch Road		Corn Exchange

LEEDS CITY TRAMS. Issued subject to the Bye-Laws. Ticket available only on Car on which issued & to Station of nearest Punch Hole. NOT TRANSFERABLE

Glasgow Numerical Printing Co.

This is a typical tram ticket of the 1940s. Each value of ticket was in different colour to indicate the various prices and these would be held in place by spring clips on a wooden board which had a leather strap underneath so it could be held securely by the conductor in his hand without slipping out.

He also carried a leather satchel with a large flap over the front with a strap around his shoulder, so the satchel was always in front of his chest. The satchel contained different compartments for each value of coin or note.

The conductor would punch a hole in the ticket to signify the destination. Every time he punched the ticket, it rang a bell, and this is the reason the conductors were called 'clippies'. An inspector would frequently board the tram to check the correct tickets had been issued.

In the early morning, I would travel to school together with the workers who would be smoking their Woodbine or Park Drive cigarettes which would be stuck between their lips so they could hold their copy of the Daily Mirror in both hands.

They would inhale the smoke from their cigarettes, at the same time, pushing the excess smoke from their face by pushing air down their nose and creating volumes of thick sickly smoke, and occasionally having their early morning smoker's cough, with the unpleasant prospect of spitting to clear their throat, but a notice in bold letters read 'No Spitting' and threatened a fine of £5 for any infringement.

I always climbed the circular stairs to get the best view of the passing scenery. If you could get a seat at the front, you would sometimes see a cyclist with his wheels stuck in the tram lines, and whether he had his front or rear wheel in the track, or both, would determine his gyrations. It was unfortunate, but you just had to laugh at other people's misfortune, especially when you'd experienced the same death-defying gyrations yourself. It certainly was very frightening, especially if you heard a tram on the tracks behind you. The experienced cyclist would brake sharply and lift his cycle out of the track – that's if he hadn't already fallen over in the process.

For my amusement during the journey, I would play a little game of guessing the occupations of each traveller. The man in old clothes with heavy boots and string tied around his trousers was probably a gardener, who probably had the same reason as the road menders that their tied-up trousers was to prevent rats climbing up their trouser legs.

I had a list in my mind of possible occupations which included lady shop assistants, male office workers and salesmen, who usually looked quite smart in their 'Fifty Shilling Tailors' suit. Many of course in Leicester worked in the hosiery or boot and shoe industries. These workers were comparatively well paid at a time when Leicester was reputed to be one of the wealthiest cities in Europe.

Advertisement – *Morgan Squires invite you to visit their 'MAKE-DO AND MEND' Exhibition. Open daily at 11 am to 3 pm. Special Advice Bureau, Hotel Street Leicester.*

Having been drilled by the necessity to make things last longer during the war, I still practice this philosophy today. I dislike disposing of things which may have their life extended by a little bit of tinkering. I have a favourite pair of shoes which I've glued the soles back to make them last a bit longer. If I was to write another book, it would be on how to 'Make Do and Mend'.

Another amusing advert of the time was for Zubes Cough Sweets – *Showing a picture of a horse, with the question: Horse? Then Go suck a Zube! These were not rationed, so we used them as ordinary sweets.*

One unrationed treat was the sweet-tasting malt loaf, which was very dark in colour and brick-shaped, although somewhat smaller in size. I would go to the baker's, eat the whole loaf, and then return home to enjoy my tea!

Shortly after we left Littlehampton, Allied forces landed on the beaches of France on 6th June. My father's 30 Assault Unit, comprising 120 men, landed a couple of days later, on different days, with three separate missions.

Before they embarked, whilst still based in Littlehampton, they were warned by Ian Fleming: *"You can't behave like 'Red Indians' any more. You have to learn to be a respected and disciplined unit."* This was prompted by many previous acts of indiscipline, understandably caused by men letting off steam after taking part in extremely dangerous missions.

Another reason for his warning was that he knew the unit was going to be fighting with American forces in their assault on Cherbourg, whilst passing through German lines, and didn't want to become any more unpopular than they already were with the American top brass for their unconventional methods of obtaining intelligence.

The following order was given to the fighting men of this unit:

"The necessity for avoiding or eliminating witnesses to successful action is emphasised."

It's quite clear what this meant and explains the 'Licence to Kill' used by Ian Fleming in his James Bond books, Fleming being the person who gave this order in the first place.

This confirms my belief, backed up by my conversations with men of the unit, that the marine was shot dead after he was heard telling people in a pub about the work of the unit.

After landing on Utah beach, my father's troop headed for the town of Sainte-Mère-Église and camped in a field close to the town.

After bedding down for the night, they heard a plane flying overhead and took no notice, assuming it was one of their own. However, this was not the case and my father described what happened next in vivid detail.

Firstly, he told me, they heard an explosion in the sky above them, then a strange fluttering noise, followed by a few seconds of quiet and then another almighty explosion and flashes sounding like machine-gun fire.

The bomb had split into many different parts and spread over a wide area with one exploding very close to him. He said he'd been very lucky to be uninjured, whilst another man standing only a few yards away was killed instantly. One other marine was killed, with 20 more casualties.

They would all have been prepared for any ground attack, but had never expected such an unusual air attack as this. This came as a wake-up call to be prepared for the unexpected, and came as quite a shock to all the marines.

The unit had been given three objectives, all planned before the invasion, to obtain important intelligence.

The first group of men, a small taskforce, landed on Juno beach, headed for the Radar station at Douvres-la-Délivrande, which they quickly captured and carried away much useful intelligence.

The second small group were tasked with capturing the V1 rocket site which had been identified by American intelligence. They passed through dense woods and eventually came across the site only to find it deserted. They looked around but couldn't find much and called up the experts who claimed it contained a lot of useful information.

The third and main force, in which my father was involved, was tasked with the capture of the German (*Kriegsmarine*) Naval Headquarters in Cherbourg to gather important intelligence. This target had been identified by the French Resistance and passed to London.

Together with the assistance of American 6th Infantry Division soldiers, the unit drove quickly through the middle of the Cherbourg Peninsular, through the German lines, and in advance of the main Allied force. They captured the Naval Headquarters and obtained a vast amount of useful intelligence, which was sent back to London and used against the German army for the remainder of the war in Europe. This would have been very useful information so early in the campaign, helping to defeat the enemy.

I saw photographs of the captured head-quarters, with the bodies of dead German soldiers lying about in the street, probably killed by the same men whom I'd met on many occasions, during and after the war, but they never seemed like killers to me!

Although the operations of 30 AU were generally kept secret, the captured intelligence had a significant effect on shortening the length of the war.

This unit never took the 'Geneva Convention' regarding the rules of war very seriously. They simply did whatever was necessary to obtain the specified intelligence. Both sides broke the rules to suit their own circumstances.

One incident which occurred on 12th September of 1944 in Dieppe could certainly be described as beyond anyone's understanding of a reasonable military code of conduct.

30 Assault Unit's Captain 'Peter' Huntington-Whitely was leading a patrol of Marine Commandos intending to take the surrender of the German garrison in that town, and had been told that resistance was unlikely.

As he approached the area, he was met by a group of German soldiers wishing to surrender, so he sent some of his party to take them to a nearby camp and was left with just three other marines to carry out his task.

Shortly afterwards, they were approached by more German soldiers carrying a white flag and wishing to surrender, but as they were about to take them into custody, they came under heavy machine-gun fire, which was aimed at all the group, including the German prisoners. Huntington-Whitely, aged 24, and Marine Geoffrey Shaw, aged 22, were shot dead, but the other two Marines managed to withdraw uninjured.

The conduct of the sniper was typical of the fanatical Nazi who'd been indoctrinated with hatred for any opposition to the Nazi cause, which, in this case, even included his own surrendering soldiers.

The loss of Huntington-Whitely was felt by all his battle-hardened colleagues. I know my father was terribly upset. This man was the ultimate hero's hero and as already noted, he was the man most likely to have been the model for Ian Fleming's James Bond.

It's strange to recall that he'd survived the raid on this same town in 1942, which could be described as a far more dangerous mission than the one in which he was killed.
My father remarked to me after the war about the terrible irony of this town, with its first three letters being 'die', taking his friend in 1944, together with hundreds of Canadian troops in the Dieppe raid of 1942. This was an appropriate epitaph for the town.

One of 30 AU's missions ended in disaster. A truck carrying two captured German torpedoes exploded when bumping over a booby-trapped level crossing, killing the two occupants and throwing them onto a live mine field.

A second truck and accompanying jeeps could not stop to recover the bodies from such a dangerous location.

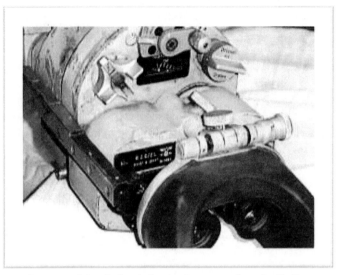

On one of my father's home leaves, after the D-Day landings, he'd returned home with these huge binoculars which he'd looted from a German naval gun battery in Cherbourg.
They had filters, so you could look directly into the sun and see the sun spots. They also had filters for looking through the mist and filters for various other kinds of weather conditions. You could see close-up for many miles. They were so powerful.

1945

Most intelligence gathering operations had been pre-determined by the 'back-room boys' from information gathered before any operation took place, to provide targets for each troop to explore after exhaustive enquiries from different intelligence sources had been made, including the French Resistance, SOE spies in enemy-occupied countries, and some secret information from Bletchley Park.

These targets were all included in what was called 'The Black Book' but in some instances, intelligence was collected by the sleuthing of commanders in the field.

One such major capture of intelligence towards the end of the war was achieved by Lt Commander 'Sancho' Glanville. Whilst searching for technical and operational information, he came across a German signal, with copy addresses at a place called Tambach, a name unknown to him, but which he found on his map and discovered it was a Schloss, so he and his men went to locate this castle. On arrival, they were confronted by a German Naval sentry at the gate and demanded "Take us to the Admiral" with no idea if any officers were still in the building.

The sentry replied, "Which one? There are three Admirals."

What they'd discovered was the entire German Naval Archives, including all the personal notes of Admiral Doenitz's top-level meetings with Hitler. This information was wired back to Ian Fleming in London who immediately ordered Glanville to shoot all three Admirals (A Licence to Kill).

He declined this order from his superior officer with the retort, "I have done some pretty rum things in this war, but I draw the line at shooting unarmed prisoners."

Following this discovery, tons of secret material was returned to the Admiralty in London for evaluation.

My father, on the right-hand side of the picture, celebrating with his men, after the defeat of Nazi Germany. This picture was taken at the German Military Barracks at Minden.

Once 30 Assault Unit had returned from Minden, Germany, after the end of hostilities, they relocated their headquarters to Guildford in Surrey, ready to disband. So, whilst I was visiting, I was told I could ride this Excelsior Welbike folding motor cycle, used by Special Forces and airborne troops. You had to push the bike to start the engine then off I sped around the extensive grounds at top speed. As a twelve-year-old boy, I thought I'd arrived in heaven!

One of the most significant achievements of 30 AU was to capture three of the most important German scientists: Wernher von Braun, his brother and Walter Dornberger in Bavaria, whom they handed over to the American Forward Intelligence Unit, and who subsequently worked on the development of the American Space Programme.

They also captured Professor Martin, the V2 rocket fuel chemist, who was also handed over to the Americans; the German Naval dockyards in Bremen together with five U-Boats and two destroyers; a huge amount of technical information on all types of weaponry, jet and rocket planes, V weapons, guided bombs, torpedoes and mines; many top-ranking military and naval personnel some of whom may have been 'questioned' by my German-speaking father; Admiral Doenitz, who'd become Führer after Hitler's death and many other intelligence secrets gathered during various campaigns, which will probably never be revealed.

Another mission by 30 AU was to drive into the Russian Sector of Berlin to bring back one of the German scientists' wives, who they dressed in disguise as an ATS female soldier to be reunited with her husband.

Latest news – Lancaster Bomber Crash.

On the afternoon of Sunday, 8th April 1945, at 3:15 in the afternoon (just a few weeks before the end of the war in Europe), I was in my garden in Bushby. I climbed the fence at the bottom of our garden to watch a Lancaster bomber, which had flown from the Heavy Conversion Unit based at North Luffenham airfield.

It was accompanied by two Spitfires, which were practising attacking manoeuvres in what was described as 'a fighter affiliation exercise' against the bomber, whilst the pilot of the Lancaster, under training supervision for conversion from flying medium bombers to qualify as a heavy-bomber pilot, before being posted to an operational squadron. The air gunner in the Lancaster simply practised firing at the Spitfires.

The pilot, under instruction, was required to make manoeuvres by tossing and turning his aircraft to avoid being shot down by the practising 'enemy' Spitfire fighter planes.

The instructor would direct the pilot to make every move to the limit to avoid being shot down which would be a matter of life and death in a real attack.

I watched in disbelief as the Lancaster started to slowly descend towards the ground. The pilot appeared to lose control of the bomber, as I watched it fly lower and lower over Station Road, about half a mile away from my home.

Then I saw a huge explosion as the plane crashed into a field with a frightening thunderous noise. As it hit the ground a plume of black smoke rose hundreds of feet into the air.

I immediately ran down the garden, collected my bike, and pedalled as hard as I could down Uppingham Road and into Station Road, not knowing what I expected to find or even if I could have helped. On the left-hand side, a few hundred yards further down the road, I dropped my bike on the grass verge and climbed over a gate and into a field.

I stood there in the field alone. I was transfixed by the terrible scene of carnage. There was a raging fire in the long deep crater, which set off the blank shells from what was left of the gun turrets.

The sight I witnessed was terrible for a twelve-year-old to see. What was left of the bodies of the poor souls was scattered around. These bright young airmen were no more. Their young heroic lives ended.

I soon returned home with the awful memory of what I'd seen and couldn't get the terrible picture from my mind for a long time. No doubt this kind of nightmare was repeated many times throughout the course of the war among soldiers and civilians who'd witnessed the dreadful sights of war.

The six men who died as I witnessed this tragedy were: Warrant Officer Ralf Wingrove, Wireless Operator, aged 24; Norman Cook, pilot, aged 23; Gerald Gore, Air Gunner, aged 20; Sergeant Jack Winterbottom, Pilot aged 24; Sergeant James Stanley, Air Gunner, aged 20 and Thomas Nea, Air Bomber, aged 22.

Ralf Wingrove had been in service with the RAF since before the war started. They were all so young to die, especially having so nearly survived this close to the end of the war.

IN MEMORY OF

THE CREW WHO DIED WHEN

R.A.F. LANCASTER ND647 of 1653.HCU.UNIT

CRASHED & EXPLODED 30yds.LEFT OF THIS SPOT

3.15pm.Sunday April 8th.1945

— o —

W/O Ralf Wingrove (Wireless op.)24yrs.
F/O Norman Cook(Pilot)23yrs.   Sgt Gerald Gore (Air Gunner)20yrs.
Sgt.Jack Winterbottom (Pilot)24yrs.

Sgt.James Stanley (Air Gunner)20yrs.

F/O Thomas Neale (Air Bomber)22yrs.

— o —

LEST WE FORGET

This plaque, in memory of those who died in the plane crash I witnessed claims to be a short distance away from the crash site. This is incorrect, however. It was at least a quarter of a mile in a south-east direction from where this is sited in Drumcliffe Road.
It was just a short distance lower down Station Road, below where the Swallow pub is situated today.

Latest News – Monday 7th May 1945 – The end of the war in Europe announced.

I remember exactly where I was on this historic day, Victory in Europe, VE Day. I was playing in a field behind the Rose and Crown public house in Thurnby with my pals, and close to where my friend Doug's sister lived in a caravan. Suddenly, she threw open the door and shouted as loud as she could: "The war's over!" which resulted in much shouting of our own, and dancing around until we were quite exhausted. You cannot imagine our joy and excitement after having suffered the perils and hardships of six years of war. Then we sat down and made plans for how we would celebrate this memorable occasion.

We settled on lighting a bonfire at night, as this would not have been allowed at any time during the whole of the war because of the 'blackout'.

When it was getting dark, Doug and I assembled at our friend Ted's house and prepared to light the bonfire. At the top of his garden, we prepared the twigs which we set up nicely in a heap in anticipation of this memorable occasion, but, after many attempts to light the fire, it determinedly refused to cooperate. This was probably due to it having rained earlier in the day, but we suffered this failure with equanimity and a stiff upper lip as we'd learned to do during the war, but this disappointment could not diminish our joy at the ending of the war in Europe, after years of conflict.

We expected everything to change quickly now that the war in Europe was over, but it was to be some time before conditions returned to normal and rationing of food continued in various degrees for a few years.

The cost of the war had almost crippled Britain, so we had to be bailed out by the United States by borrowing huge sums of money through what was called the Marshall Plan which took many years to repay.

After Big Ben had struck three on the afternoon of 8th May, Mr Churchill broadcast from the BBC that the war in Europe will end officially at 12.01 pm the next day, although the ceasefire order was given the day before; however, this agreement will be ratified in Berlin that day. Mr Churchill concluded his broadcast with the warning that we now needed to finish the war against Japan.

For the first time since the war began, it was possible to tell the world what weather Britain was expecting. That day, all restrictions were removed by the censors. The first weather forecast since the outbreak of war was issued by the Air Ministry early in the afternoon. Light or moderate, variable or easterly winds, mainly fine at first, scattered thunderstorms and thundery rain later in the day, and in the night; warm (Weather forecasts were not made public during the war because it could have assisted German military operations against Britain).

It was reported in the newspapers that they will not publish their editions the next day, 9th May, in common with other newspapers. This was in accordance with the expressed desire of the Government that workers should enjoy a day's holiday following the cessation of hostilities in Europe.

Shortly before 30 AU disbanded after the end of the war, a group of about thirty officers and senior NCOs had a farewell 'get-together' which was also attended by Ian Fleming. My father had a chat with him and he told him that he intended to write about his war-time experiences, although it was to be a few years before he started writing the James Bond novels.

So, who was James Bond? It's my belief that the character was based, principally, on the six-feet three-inch Captain 'Peter' Huntington-Whitely, known as 'Red' amongst his colleagues.

He was a Royal Marines Commando Lieutenant at the age of just 22, and was selected by Ian Fleming to be the first officer of the newly formed intelligence-gathering unit of 30 Commando and was responsible for the initial interviews for selection to this unit.

He was well known to Ian Fleming because they'd co-operated together in the failed attempt to 'pinch' an Enigma de-coding machine during the Dieppe raid.

They were both Old Etonians, and it's quite possible they were known to each other before the war even started, because both families were part of the wealthy upper-class social set in London.

Huntington-Whitely's grandfather was the former British Prime Minister, Stanley Baldwin, so he already had an impressive pedigree.

Ian Fleming, a member of the wealthy Fleming banking dynasty, had had a comfortable war, enjoying a wide circle of affluent friends and wining and dining at the best London restaurants. He also enjoyed the company of many attractive women, and has been described as a bit of a 'ladies'' man. However, this does not detract from his achievements as originator and commander of this elite fighting unit. So, in this respect, Ian Fleming's own life-style would have been a perfect match for James Bond and much of his own lifestyle is portrayed in his James Bond novels.

The character of Miss Moneypenny is reputed to be based on Miss Margaret Priestley, a Leeds University history don who worked for Ian Fleming and played an important role in the running and administration of 30 AU.

My belief is that Captain 'Peter' Huntington-Whitely is the principal model for James Bond. He was Fleming's most trusted officer, well known for his courage and bravery and was the perfect fit for the character of James Bond.

SORTIE BOMBING RECORD

Sortie No.	Year / Date	Individual (Day) Target	Time	Type	No.	Date	Target a/c	Time 10,000 feet / 1,000 feet	Type	Serial No.	Drill	Moving Target — Low Level	Actual Finish Time	Comd. Officer's Signature and Remarks
1	27.3.42	ROUEN	4.05	WHITLEY	21	24.7.43	HANOVER	5.30		41	4.5.44	CALAIS	1.50	
2	W.5.42	R.S.B.R. Patrol	9.40		22	25.7.43	MANNHEIM	5.55		42	8.5.44	ALENCON	4.45	
3	7.5.42		7.45		23	28.7.43	KASSEL	5.40		43	8.6.44	OISEMONT	3.50	
4	14.5.42		9.00		24	29.7.43	MANNHEIM	6.10		44	7.7.44	CAEN	3.25	
5	16.5.42		9.45		25	30.7.43	LEVERKUSEN	5.20		45	12.7.44	VRAIRES	4.00	
6	17.5.42		7.30		26	2.8.43	BERLIN	6.30		46	14.7.44	REVIGNY	7.40	
7	22.5.42		10.15		27	23.8.43	FRANKFURT	6.25		47	15.7.44	NUCOURT	4.00	
8	13.11.43	AACHEN	5.55	MANUF	28	31.8.43	MAGDEBURG	4.30		48	18.7.44	WESSELING	2.50	
9	16.11.43	MONTBELIARD	7.50		29	3.11.43	HELIGOLAND	4.20		49	20.7.44	ARDOUVAL	3.10	
10	8.11.43	HAMBURG	4.10		30	20.11.43	BERLIN	7.15		50	23.7.44	KIEL	5.20	
11	23.11.43	ESSEN	5.10		31	26.11.43	BERLIN	6.45		51	8.7.44	STUTTGART	7.30	
12	7.11.43	HANNOVER	4.10		32	2.12.43	BERLIN	6.35		52	25.7.44	STUTTGART	7.40	
13		HAMBURG	4.40		33	16.12.43	STUTTGART	4.20		53	8.8.44	PRUILLAC	1.45	
14	10.11.43	RAMSTEID	4.05		34	18.12.43	FRANKFURT	4.50		54	7.8.44	CAEN	3.10	
15	23.11.43	HANNOVER	9.00		35	24.3.44	BERLIN	6.25		55	11.8.44	LENS	3.30	
16	18.11.43	NURENBORG	9.05		36	30.3.44	NUREMBERG	7.00		56	9.8.44	N° FALAISE	3.15	
17	5.11.43	MANNHEIM	4.10		37	11.4.44	MAILLY	3.45		57	15.8.44	GRESSICOURT	3.00	
18	11.11.43	COLOGNE	3.00		38	4.5.44	FT GRASSICOURT	3.10		58	11.8.44	STETTIN	7.25	
19	19.11.43	NEUFLUSSON	5.45		39	19.5.44	ORLEANS	4.25		59	18.8.44			
20	11.11.43	MODANE	7.00		40	21.3.44	MONT-COUPLE	4.00						

c/f 158:10   4/625:40   TOTAL No. OF HOURS 332:10

TOTAL No. OF SORTIES   51

* DAYLIGHT SORTIES *

On the previous page is a copy of the bombing record of the father of one of my friends. In an age of heroes, it is quite exceptional in that the requisite number of sorties was exceeded by 21 missions, especially when you consider the normal life expectation for a bomber crew was much less than 30 required sorties. In all, over 50,000 bomber crew lost their lives during the conflict.

Furthermore, this crew survived the notorious Nuremberg raid, when so many Lancaster bombers were shot down because the raid was carried out on a moon-lit night, providing the German fighter planes with easy targets to shoot down.

My father's Certificate of Commando War Service.

Latest News – my mother saw this advert and decided to go shopping!

Morgan Squires, Hotel Street, Leicester – *For the Junior Miss. Styled in check fibre and beautifully tailored, the frock illustrated is particularly designed for the Junior Miss. Colours cherry blue and green. 7 clothing coupons. Forty-one shillings and five pence (just over two pounds).*

Herringtons, Market Street, Leicester – *Good selection of handbags in the latest styles from nine shillings and eleven pence. Just under 50 pence!*

After the war ended and the servicemen returned to civilian life, they took over many of the jobs that women had done during the war. Women had played a huge role in the war effort during those years.

One of my father's colleagues in the Royal Marines, Johnny Kruthhoffer, visited us with his newly married, attractive, blonde-haired wife, Eva, who told us about her experiences as fire crew during the Blitz in London in 1940. I hadn't realised that women were involved in such dangerous work. She remarked that she had to wear trousers as fire-engine drivers tended to get fresh with the ladies, even in those hazardous situations.

When members of the armed forces were demobbed at the end of hostilities, they were given a war gratuity and post war credits; my father's payment amounted to 76 pounds and 18 shillings. Also, they were given a suit of clothes: jacket, trousers, waistcoat and trilby hat, supposedly from Montague Burton, the high-street tailors. Hence the term: 'The Full Monty'. They were of questionable quality and you could recognise any ex-serviceman wearing these clothes, as they never seemed to fit very well.

After my dad was demobbed from the forces, he applied for a disabled pension because his legs had open wounds caused by having desert sores which refused to heal, but after a medical he was turned down, to my absolute disgust. This suffering lasted to the end of his life. That's the gratitude he received for serving his country so bravely.

The men of my father's unit were trained killers in pursuit of their objectives, it's what they'd been trained to do and, although they carried out these killings, I've no doubt many of the men suffered the effects after the war ended. I know it affected my father, who also deeply felt the loss of close colleagues who'd lost their lives in battle. A few years after the war ended, sadly, he was to take his own life.

This kind of treatment had been going on for hundreds of years. Even from the time of Lord Nelson's battle of Trafalgar, wounded sailors and marines were discharged from their ships, and left to fend for themselves.

After the First World War, gassed, blinded and legless soldiers were forced to beg on the streets and sell matches. Even in this modern 'civilised' age, wounded soldiers are left to use the NHS once discharged from the forces with no special privileges after having loyally served their country.

If I'd had the choice, I wouldn't have chosen to encounter a world war at the age of six, but that was the situation, so it couldn't be avoided.

As a seven-year old, the war started in earnest, and we all feared being invaded. All we school children were instructed on using our gas masks and finding our way to the air-raid shelters. Sweets were rationed, and food shortages prevented us from enjoying some of our favourite foods. I loved lots of butter on my bread, but this was soon restricted to very thin scrapes.

For the next five years, I was at school with elderly teachers, who were not required to serve in the forces and didn't seem wholly dedicated to the task of teaching unruly school boys. Their lack of enthusiasm was eagerly embraced by boys of my ability, who were more interested in adventure and sport. The pilot Biggles of comic fame and Dick Barton, Special Agent, were two of my fictional heroes.

As children growing up in the war, most of our lives revolved around matters related to the progress of the war, which the whole family followed with an avid interest, as if our lives depended on it, which of course they did.

Strange to think now that our young lives, during those years, were so involved with death and destruction.

What of the men of 30 Assault Unit, who I came to know so well and who'd been involved in the most dangerous of missions, not only on the front line, but also intelligence-gathering assaults into enemy territory?

They faced torture and death if caught by the Germans, but they seemed quite unfazed by this prospect, and had a 'devil-may-care' attitude to danger. No doubt they intended to live life to the full, whilst it lasted, not knowing how long that may be. These men didn't appear to me to be any different to other soldiers I'd met, but courage is something inside the man. He doesn't wear it on his chest.

These men were prepared to sacrifice their own lives for what they believed was a just cause.

After the war I had the pleasure of meeting and spending some time with Leonard Cheshire VC, who was so modest and unassuming, as was typical of the other heroes I met previously.

Dancing in the streets

AN ARMY sergeant swings his beret for a party hat as he joins revellers dancing the conga round Leicester's Clock Tower during the VE Day celebrations.

It was typical of scenes throughout Leicestershire as thousands thronged the streets for celebrations that lasted two days and nights.

Many others flocked to the parks, while the youngsters tucked in at street parties.

There were fireworks in the Market Place and floodlights and coloured lights lit up the Town Hall, an emphatic reminder that the blackouts were over.

VE Day – put out the flags!

It's impossible to describe the excitement following the announcement of the end of hostilities in Europe. This picture shows how people were enjoying the moment by dancing around the Clock Tower in Leicester.

Patriotism and pride in our country was a common characteristic of the people of Britain during the war. Regrettably, this is much less so nowadays.

If we were faced with a similar situation to that which we faced in 1939, I don't believe we'd find the same degree of loyalty and dedication to our country again, with the growth of our multi-cultural society.

This war had been a long and difficult journey of hardships, fear, tragedy and sorrow, but finally, also of relief and joy at reaching the end of this long winding road.